ASIAN AFFAIRS DIVISION

Fragments of a Revolution

Fragments of a Revolution

ESSAYS ON INDIAN PROBLEMS

by

M. CHALAPATHI RAU

PERGAMON PRESS
OXFORD · LONDON · EDINBURGH · NEW YORK
PARIS · FRANKFURT

Pergamon Press Ltd., Headington Hill Hall, Oxford
4 & 5 Fitzroy Square, London W.1

Pergamon Press (Scotland) Ltd., 2 & 3 Teviot Place, Edinburgh 1

Pergamon Press Inc., 44-01 21st Street, Long Island City, New York 11101

Permagon Press S.A.R.L 24 rue des Ecoles, Paris 5e

Pergamon Press GmbH, Kaiserstrasse 75, Frankfurt-am-Main

First edition 1965

Library of Congress Catalog Card No. 65–26879

PRINTED IN GREAT BRITAIN
BY THE CARRICK PRESS LTD.

2360/65

To JAWAHARLAL NEHRU, who among other things was a great teacher, who taught me much

Contents

Preface

THIS is a collection of essays on Indian problems. They are all present problems and have an underlying unity. It is the unity of India and of her integration, which is a continuing process. In social and economic terms, it is a revolutionary process, and the essays deal with many aspects of the revolution, which, in spite of its silences, is real. For two generations, the Indian Revolution, first under Gandhi's and then under Jawaharlal Nehru's leadership, has been going on, but it is still in a somewhat fragmentary form and is here dealt with in a rather fragmentary fashion.

This is not a treatise or a thesis. The essay form has enabled the writer to adopt an easy, confident manner; he has written as a commentator rather than as a chronicler and has criticized freely many aspects of Indian life, but with a sense of responsibility to history. Each essay can stand by itself; together, the essays are intended to present a comprehensive, not detailed, picture of the troubled processes of the revolution. The claim is to consistency of outlook, whether the problem is political, constitutional, social, cultural or religious. The approach is serious, but the treatment, it is hoped, is not heavy for the general reader in India or elsewhere.

M. CHALAPATHI RAU

New Delhi,
1 January 1965

1. Five Thousand Years

THE mounds of Mohenjo-doro reveal a five-thousand-year-old civilization with many millenniums of human endeavour behind it and in some respects superior to that of contemporary Mesopotamia and Egypt. From Mohenjo-doro to the modern nation state of India, it has been a recurring, centuries-long crisis. Marshall, Mortimer Wheeler and other archaeologists have drawn explanations from the dug-outs of antiquity and Toynbee has tried to trace the behaviour of civilizations. The continuity and oneness of the many processes which have made India what she is, changing yet unageing, are now easily explained. The inundations of Central Asian peoples through the north-western passes, of Iranians, Greeks, Parthians, Bactrians, Scythians, Huns, Turks, Jews, Zoroastrians, and Muslims, forces ranging from primitive communism to myth and ritual, many philosophies, many religions contributed to the making of India. These layers upon layers of thought and experience have absorbed much research by scholars in the raw material of history. Yet a broad outline makes more sense than crowded dates and genealogy, for there is a congestion of cultural forms, in spite of several blank pages, in Indian history.

" What is India ? " asked Jawaharlal Nehru again and again. Is it the *Upanishads*, the great epics, the Gita, the Buddha and other manifestations of the human spirit, taken together or separately ? It is all these and more, ignorance, enlightenment, the din of schisms, clamorous creeds, the coming of St. Thomas, the impact of Islam, and what British civil servants and historians called benefits of British rule. Every century is represented in this country, and nearly fifty centuries heavily hang over it. There are long periods of silence which descend like a curtain on yet undeciphered dark ages. It is unprofitable to take refuge in the real or unreal golden ages of the past, for that would be a reaction in favour of revivalism. It is better to look " forward to the future and backwards to the past", and then there is the present with its problems. If India is what she is, how far will she accept change and what will she be in the centuries ahead?

India is no longer lonely in the world. The ferment of the age has thrown up metaphysical groups, Marxist and non-Marxist, without a Donne, and the new scholasticism has not found its Dante. *Paradise Lost* included contemporary cosmogeny in a neat and compact form, and other ages have produced their epics, beside which we have yet only doggerel in life and literature. The rapid advances in technology make this age terrific in its promise. Social and economic change is fast and modes and means of production are transformed rapidly. The social distribution of power is a pressing problem. Science is embarrassingly exciting and humanizing. Eras are telescoped and man has reached the frontiers of outer space. The primacy of matter and the inevitability of change are not mere slogans of the new materialism. There is change, there is continuity, there is the new amidst the old.

The Indian Revolution reflects this temper. Like other revolutions, it is compounded of its own renaissances and reformations, and is a process, not an event. Gandhi and Jawaharlal Nehru were a part of this process, but neither has yet been placed in a historical setting. Gandhi has to be given his place in the broad stream of national consciousness as a social and economic revolutionary and reassessed, divorced from the martyr's manner of his death. He was a part of the historical process and should not be hidden in the grey eminence of a greatness reduced to a legend. Jawaharlal Nehru also should not be similarly lost.

The nation-building process goes on at many levels. The revolution is not yet total in character, and those who understand the processes can still master them. If life is real, society as a whole should base itself on acceptance of life, not on renunciation, which has had a long tradition in India. It must be the whole of life, for the future is unfolding too rapidly. In an age of rapid transformation, a " new base of civilization, fitting in with technology, will be gradually erected, and with it will develop new ideologies, new forms of collective life and, indeed, a broader philosopy of life." To welcome the future so ardently, freedom from fear is necessary, but fear prevails in the present, tense, conflict-ridden world. Peace, which to some is now merely a dove painted by Picasso, will mean more than coexistence, when the present economic systems and ideologies will be dust.

The effect of technology on a traditional society in transition like India's has already been striking. The desire for personal salvation is giving place to a sense of responsibility to social progress. There is an increase in the number of people who are participating in production on a large scale, in production by machines and not by hands, and they are now watching machines which make machines at work. Technology has not obliterated all divisions in the west and will not for a long time obliterate caste and subcaste in India, but there is no resistance to change. If there are social tensions, the struggle is not between religious beliefs and new values or between individualism and increasing forms of collectivism but rather between ancient lethargies and the dynamics of modern production and between social habits and social needs. Traditional values like tolerance, non-violence and other-worldliness, which is not outdated in these days of outer-space exploration, will not be casualties, but it will require nerve for a traditional society proud of old values to face the future, untempted by any Mephistopheles of the age.

2. Unity and Diversities

WHAT kind of integration did India ever achieve and how was it lost? For centuries India was first a legend which lived in the vision of her sages and then a river-valley civilization, without physical or political boundaries, which attracted the wandering conqueror. There were many invasions, but India absorbed the impact of every one of them; only the Turks in the early Middle Ages, and the Chagtai Mughals later, established permanent empires. Muslim conquest brought about many political and cultural changes in the old societies of India, but the foundation and structure of the old culture remained. Even the Mughal political system was founded upon a socio-economic base which retained substantial identity throughout the ancient and medieval periods till the nineteenth century.

India's racial mould, unlike that of Europe, was set once for all, from Aryan times, and was little disturbed in the succeeding centuries. Later a synthesis of the Aryan, Dravidian and aboriginal elements was formed and was little upset. The ethnic and economic base underwent the least change. So did trade and industry. Village and caste meant stability as much as stagnation. There was cultural *rapprochement* between Hinduism and Islam, but it failed to generate national consciousness and the state did not foster it. Economic and social change was slow. As the Mughal structure crumbled, the weakness of the central authority reacted upon the economic life of the state and centrifugalism and localism dominated. It was at this time that the agents of European powers intervened powerfully, interrupting more than one synthesis.

The India of the Mughals disappeared rapidly with the death of Aurangzeb. The country was a static conglomeration of villages, castes, classes, tribes and principalities loosely held together. The economy was agricultural, its technique primitive and its aim subsistence production. Industry was organized on a small scale; money played an insignificant part. In Europe it was the age of science and reason and new techniques. The consequences of the impact of the west on India have been variously assessed. It was a mixture of good and evil, the economy was organized to supply raw material for the Industrial Revolution in England, while poverty and pressure on land increased. The growth of national consciousness was a certain consequence; a renaissance was another, though it was accompanied by revivalism. The emergence of national societies is a recent stage of social development, and for a country like India which, till the end of the nineteenth century, retained conditions amounting to feudalism and even now had not eliminated semi-feudal conditions completely, the nation-building process is not easy. But it is an inevitable process.

Why did India lose independence? Did India qualify for freedom? Europe, says Dr. Tara Chand, India's leading historian, progressed from independence to freedom, from the settlements of the Teutonic tribes in the provinces of the Roman Empire to the eighteenth century, without experiencing foreign occupation and rule, while India had to surrender sovereign power and then struggle towards self-government, completing the process in one-fifth of the time taken by Europe. There is another difference between Europe and India. The achievement of freedom by India is the transformation of a civilization into nationality and the fulfilment of nationality through the establishment of national sovereignty. It was a dialectic process; the first step was the destruction of the older order culminating in 1857; the second step was the emergence of a new order which gathered momentum during the following half-century; the third step was one of conflict and synthesis and the emergence of the Indian nation state.

The political map was changing, and history books indicate Wellesley's India or Dalhousie's India, with increasing patches of red. There were many political units, but there was one broad civilization and one socio-economic structure. With territorial integrity and political sovereignty, the problem is to pull together that civilization and to adjust institutions to social and economic change. The language problem is that Indian languages are struggling to take the place of English as media of education and of expression of long-standing cultures. The states reorganization problem is that, with historical memories, old subcultures want to regain their identity as a part of the national structure. The economic problem is that there should be enough production, equitable distribution and large-scale employment opportunities. The political problem is that parties should be secular, national parties preserving the spirit of parliamentary democracy and reconciling the socialist process with the democratic process. The minorities problem is that there should be cultural safeguards and social and economic equality. These are not insuperable problems. The British were the unconscious instruments of revolution ; the Indian people have to make that revolution complete.

3. How Freedom Came

AUGUST Fifteenth, Indian Independence Day, is not what July Fourth is in the United States or July Fourteenth in France. There is a heavy sombreness about its celebration because of tragic memories and the brooding habit of centuries. It is not from poverty or a sense of austerity that the Indian people forget to cherish and honour their freedom adequately; on many other days, they indulge in festivity and show themselves to be capable of abandon. Probably, the high seriousness of the too many messages which too many leaders deliver on freedom as a burden and responsibility gives a solemn lead to people who look too much for lead. The moment of independence was painful and sanguinary, and there are still many versions of the way independence came, but whatever the versions, it freed the people of foreign rule, of the miseries of the past, of the confusion and exhaustion of a long struggle.

There were many moments of independence, according to some indefatigable controversialists. Maulana Azad, in his slender autobiography, sought to show that if the Cabinet Mission Scheme of 1946 had been accepted by the Congress, Partition could have been avoided. Partition cannot be the only criterion for judging the value or quality of independence, but Partition has been treated in many quarters as a great defeat for Indian nationalism, as an irreparable disaster or as a wholly avoidable development. If this view were correct, it would not be enough to throw the blame on the Congress; there should be a deeper probe into the underlying social and economic processes which led to Partition, whatever may have been the faults of the British, the Congress, or the Muslim League. Ultimately, history concerns itself with fundamental forces and not merely with what parties or individuals did.

To pursue the imaginative logic of Maulana Azad far enough, Partition may have been avoidable, if the British had been in a mood to part with power after the end of the First World War or at the time of the Round Table Conferences in the early 1930s. Like Maulana Azad, many leaders in those days argued that if the Montague–Chelmsford Reforms had been accepted by the Congress in 1919, the safe and slow process of transfer of power which is in operation in British colonies in Africa would have followed in India; if the Government of India Act of 1935 had been accepted, there would have been safe and leisurely progress towards dominion status and independence. But what kind of independence? In either case, freedom would have been fettered, with safeguards entrenched in the constitutional structure and duality embedded in the national structure; freedom would not have been full. The British were in no mood or position to give up their connection with the six hundred and odd princely states of India, and nationalities may have emerged from the larger communities among them. This was not the freedom which would have satisfied the elemental forces which Gandhi had released. Though Partition has left India the third largest Muslim country in the world and Indian nationalism remains composite in its character, the Indian people were struggling to statehood so that they could do what they liked with their freedom, and they accepted Partition as the secession of unwilling elements consisting of contiguous Muslim communities. They took the risk of being free even to lose that freedom.

There were many who looked upon freedom as an anticlimax to the freedom movement. But critics of Indian freedom, who criticize freedom without criticizing the nationalist movement and criticize the Congress without criticizing Gandhi who largely made it what it was, are guilty of a contradiction. In invoking the forces of freedom, Gandhi knew he was invoking much that was good and much that was bad which had to be made good by feats of endurance, vision and leadership. His direct action could not but provoke direct action from others; his fasting was bound to be followed widely.

There was reaction and imitation. He is now scripture, but merely to quote him is to be holistic but unhistorical. Much that has happened and has been happening is a reaction to Gandhi, and it is a measure of his greatness.

Gandhi's non-violence, for instance, has been assessed as a creed of his own making and as the expression of national tradition. It was also a reaction to the character of British imperialism, which had its own non-violent processes. Foreign rule is the rule of force and not of consent, but by establishing High Courts, universities and legislatures, howsoever powerless and unrepresentative, the British established some semblance of the rule of law and civilization. To Hitlerism, even India would have reacted with open revolt and an underground of violence. The subtler forces of British rule led to a subtle movement of non-violence. Gandhi alone, among the national leaders, tried to remember the reality behind the appearance and led an uncompromising revolt against the hold of British civilization, more than that of British economic and political processes, on Indian life. Freedom came in the context of these major circumstances. It did not come with a bang; it came along with much pain, but it came and it was freedom. It is useless to criticize it for not coming more violently than it did.

4. Congress: 1885–1964

THE beginnings of the Indian National Congress in retrospect look like a Victorian burlesque; its leaders made obsequious references to Providence, and loudly swore their loyalties to the Queen Empress. The first meeting took place at noon on Monday, 28 December, 1885, in Bombay, in the great hall of the Gokuldas Tejpal Sanskrit College. The representatives, distinguished, venerable and whiskered in some cases, sat amidst a mixed gathering of officials and leading citizens. There were Woomesh Chandra Bonnerjee, the first president and first Indian Standing Counsel in a Chartered High Court; Dadabhai Naoroji, a member of the Parliament at Westminster, to be known later as the Grand Old Man of India and to preside over the Congress for three terms; and Allan Octavian Hume, the Father of the Congress, who had refused a lieutenant-governorship to be free to serve the people. There were also the president of the Eurasian Association, the Collector of Madras, Mahadev Ranade, then a judge of the Small Causes Court, Poona; and R. G. Bhandarkar, of the Decan College. It was a modest gathering of mild-mannered people, whose loyalty was equal to their patriotism.

The subjects discussed were to become stale through the years; in 1885 they were fresh. There was to be an inquiry into the working of the Indian administration by a Royal Commission; the Council of the Secretary of State, as it was then constituted, was to be abolished; the Imperial Legislative Council at Delhi and the Legislative Councils in the presidency towns were to be reformed and expanded, with the right of interpellation and submission of budgets to the councils; examination for the Civil Service was to be held both in India and in Britain; the military expenditure was to be reduced ; import duties on cotton were to be reimposed and the Licence Tax extended, together with an imperial guarantee for the Indian debt. The founding fathers of the Congress held a brief for Burma ; they asked for its separation from the India Viceroyalty. The proceedings might seem innocuous eighty years later and the resolutions may have been passed with bated breath, but it was the first organized attack on British control over the political structure, the economic policies and the administration. The session lasted for three days, there was a vote of thanks to the president, " three cheers " for Hume, and when Hume called for " three times three cheers " for her Majesty the Queen Empress, there was a demonstrative outburst of loyalty which would have amused even that sedate being commemorated so much in marble throughout the country.

The history of the Congress has been written and rewritten, and has been interpreted in various ways, including the merciless Marxist way. Some obscure points have, however, remained obscure. It is little known that the political movement was accompanied by an economic movement and by a social movement, which the leaders wanted to be left to the several major communities so that they could be brought together easily on a common platform for political reform. The Social Conference was started in 1888, and while political pioneers established economic projects ranging from soap to steel, the Industrial Conference was inaugurated in 1904. The Congress Constitution of 1908, amended in 1911 and 1912, stated in Article 1 :

> The objects of the Indian National Congress are the attainment by the people of India of a system of government similar to that enjoyed by the self-governing members of the British Empire and participation by them in the rights and responsibilities of the Empire on equal terms with those members. These objects are to be achieved by constitutional means by bringing about a steady reform of the existing system of administration and by promoting national unity, fostering public spirit and developing and organizing the intellectual, moral, economic and industrial resources of the country.

The Congress has accomplished, with impressive irony, the first of these objectives. India is free and stays within an empire converted into a commonwealth. But the objectives of " promoting national unity, fostering public spirit and developing and organizing the intellectual, moral, economic and industrial resources of the country" have yet to be fulfilled. In 1915 Ambika Charan Mazumdar, to preside over the Lucknow session a few years later, could call his history of the Congress "Indian National Evolution". Now, everyone thinks of revolution, and the question is whether the Congress is revolutionary enough.

The revolutionary phase of the Congress started with Gandhi, who released elemental forces, sometimes not knowing it. But it would be unhistorical to consign the pioneers to a portrait gallery. The poverty of the Indian people was a thesis which Dadabhai Naoroji propagated with the help of the evidence of secretaries of state. Dutt, Ranade and Gokhale carried the economic interpretation of British rule further. If the worst aspect of the regime was that the resources of the country were left undeveloped and the people were deprived of the benefits of the Industrial Revolution, the economic absorption began with Gandhi's predecessors; he invested it with urgency; and it was Jawaharlal Nehru's task to bring the temper of industrial revolution to the people and to give an economic bias to Indian understanding of progress. For some time after he became Prime Minister, Jawaharlal Nehru was not sure of his hold on the Congress; after Gandhi, it seemed he was outnumbered by those who did not believe in the policies for which he stood. But he would not leave the Congress, as his socialist friends said he should. He saw in it a mighty instrument, and when it came over to him after challenges and counter challenges in 1951, he made it his own. From the time of the Lahore Congress in 1930, he had made his impress, differing from Gandhi but working under his leadership. For fifteen years, after Gandhi, it was his Congress as wholly as it had been Gandhi's.

5. Evolution of Gandhi

GANDHI had a horror of being turned into a god, and, if he were alive, he would be 95 and would find that he is near godhood. Mummification precedes deification, and it is necessary to rescue Gandhi the man to realize, only sixteen years after his death, that such a man walked on this earth. To know Gandhi, one has to get to his beginnings, his early struggles, the ceaseless striving and experimentation by which a mere man, with modest qualities and strong appetites, evolved into a mahatma. He had not been born a mahatma. There was nothing like an incarnation of virtues assuming moral authority and sermonizing his people into feats of self-purification. From self-inquest to self-mastery, Gandhi went through a strange transfiguration ; it was an agonizing struggle, and his agonies were laid bare before the world. Most people think of Gandhi in the climax of his career and forget the preparatory years in South Africa, a fascinating period in which he was constantly working out principles and techniques which needed little change in the spacious days of the freedom struggle in India. Not only intellectually but physically, even in appearance and in manner of dress, he was changing, and there is hardly a parallel to the profusion of photographic record which illustrates this period.

Gandhi has suffered blurring in another manner. Most people forget that he was primarily not a teacher, but a rebel. To some, his greatest achievement would remain the winning of national freedom ; he annotated it into the larger social and economic freedom. It would be also useless to treat him as only a preceptor who was concerned with confession and communion. He was a political and social revolutionary, and the revolutionary forces, which he released and to which Jawaharlal Nehru gave shape, constituted the most constructive of revolutions. Any measuring of freedom merely by an act of independence or by the frustrating fact of Partition would be incomplete.

Gandhi did not seek to find a new church; he wanted no temple for himself. Yet the world has not changed much since his death, and people talk of him as if he were as remote as saints in calendars. It has been said that if Christ were to appear now, he would be crucified again; if Gandhi were to appear in India now, all the religious bigotry, communal hatred, sectarianism and social evils which still prevail would assume the shape of a bullet and kill him again. It seems a futile task for anyone to seek to foster morality, particularly political morality. This was clear to Gandhi, and he wanted not only the individual but the environment to be transformed. No one of his stature has been so caricatured as Gandhi, and the worst caricatures live in Congress ministers. Congressmen use him as their talisman without practising either truthfulness or the sense of non-possession which he held so vital for individual and national life. Opposition parties use Gandhi to criticize congressmen asking them alone to practise Gandhian principles. Conservative parties twist his theory of trusteeship and use him to support the principle of predatory self-interest. It is wrong for anyone to seek to establish a monopoly of the Gandhian heritage, and the workers who were physically close to Gandhi are probably the most acquisitive closed shop among Gandhi's followers. Gandhi deprecated the assembling of any creed from what he said or did, and to him there was no Gandhism.

The two men who were looked upon as closest to Gandhi in spirit, though in different respects, were Jawaharlal Nehru and Vinoba, and they were not monopolists. They were the two carefully selected by Gandhi in 1940 to offer Satyagraha against the war effort. Jawaharlal Nehru had later state power at his disposal and Vinoba has been mobilizing social power. Like Gandhi, they can only make an approach to the ideal, but has there been any such approach? It is easy to criticize a state or a government or even a movement by Gandhian standards, and Gandhi criticized not only his followers but himself. The people of a country like

India with an underdeveloped economy and newly won freedom may not be malleable material, but no good leader can afford to quarrel with his tools. The application of Gandhian standards is bound to be baffling too, for while Gandhi was criticized and opposed much during his lifetime, there has been almost a mechanical reverence for him after his death. Gandhian standards are becoming static rules which people use to criticize each other. If Gandhi's closest followers become a sect, they too will be incapable of exercising judgment. If all aspects of Gandhi are considered integral parts which cannot be separated, Gandhian ethics cannot be separated from Gandhian economics. The country's economy is moving away from Gandhi and is more in accord with world economy than with him. If Gandhian economics were being knocked away bit by bit under Jawaharlal Nehru's leadership, the people have to find out what part of Gandhi will be valid, apart from his uniqueness as a rebel, revolutionary and practitioner of the most excruciating truths of life.

6. Ark without Covenant

THERE was no covenant among the Indian people to make a constitution when the Constituent Assembly met, amidst controversy. It was free to draw up any constitution it liked and it deliberated fully. India's foremost lawyers and politicians took a leading part, and though there was no covenant, the Constitution has been looked upon as an ark. Many critics said that the Constitution was too long and cumbrous and might prove to be unworkable, but nobody could suggest how it could be made short and simple. By 1950 it was not possible to prepare a short and simple democratic constitution for a country like India. A short and simple, if not clear, constitution like the Soviet or Chinese Constitution is possible only with a simplified social and economic system. It is legitimate to judge the Indian Constitution by its possible economic consequences and argue that it did not provide for easy social and economic change. But till that change took place, the Constitution had to provide for existing social and economic relations, and it had also to provide for complex, and artificial, federal relations taking over many of the provisions of the Government of India Act of 1935.

The Indian Constitution was the work of many minds, most of them legal and not revolutionary minds. But nobody outside them contributed any ideas and the authorship, which must be taken to be largely anonymous, reflects political wisdom, knowledge of constitutional theory, and to an extent the dominant economic interests of the period. The possible political consequences, which are as yet inexhaustible, raise the question which Lincoln asked: must a government, of necessity, be too strong for the liberties of its own people or too weak to maintain its own existence?

The attempt to classify constitutions is unending. Under the present fashionable phraseology, the Indian Constitution provides for the parliamentary type of government as against the presidential type. The drift away from democracy in several countries takes the constitutional form of a presidential type of democracy. There have been dictators who have been voted to power through a plebiscite, but without the reality of a democratic process. The distrust which is being spread against political parties is also a trend towards the easy short cut of the dictatorship of a person, class or élite. In the search for strong governments, some Asian countries too have turned from the parliamentary executive to the non-parliamentary executive, with none of the American respect for law or fundamental rights. Republics can be amenable to bursts of ignorance and popular prejudice. Those who in the last century argued that low franchise meant slaves, not independent voters, had reason on their side and the example of Napoleon III's plebiscites. Mehemet Ali of Egypt asked what a republic was. He was told: "When Egypt becomes a republic, you will be the people, and the people could be the pashaw."

The provisions of the Indian Constitution and the corpus of conventions which become part of a constitution are frequently discussed, but the political spirit which gives meaning to constitutional provisions is being ignored. If the unwritten but implicit parliamentary pattern is not accepted, it might not only mean that a president can be impeached for misuse of power but that the president cannot carry on without the support of the majority party in Parliament. When the council of ministers is to "aid and advise" the president, it means that its "advice" has to be accepted, for political reasons, apart from the constitutional position. Confusion arises because the parliamentary system of government is not written into the Constitution; such a large constitutional practice could not be so written. Even instruments of instruction for the president and the governors would have been redundant. The Constitution, however, had superimposed on its basic parliamentary structure the fundamental rights, the power of judicial review, and the amending process. It was inevitable in a written constitution of a federal type. The result is that Indians have to draw upon both American constitutional law and British constitutional law. The parliamentary system will work only if the underlying spirit is understood and respected. In Britain, correct understanding of the role of Parliament made the difference between the Tudors and the Stuarts.

It is usually a little donkey that leads a long caravan of camels. Leadership in a young republic is important. The Indian Constitution will depend for its success not so much on the soundness of its provisions as on the temper of political parties reflecting the temper of the people. The advocacy of partyless democracy has its dangers, for the extinction of party can lead to pretentious absolutism or factionalism. Spain at one time had 60,000 people who paid attention to politics, 20,000 of them in office and the others out of office, and this was the core of Spanish politics. It might seem at times that Indian political parties have a similar flimsy basis. The threat to integration can come only from the selfishness and callousness of political parties which deny or deride what is known as the supremacy of the Constitution. It is the task of political parties to annotate the democratic process from day to day. War and absolutism have been common threats to constitutional government. The wide prevalence of jargon, which means lack of thinking, and the ignorance or irresponsibility of parties are new threats.

7. *Making of a Nation*

THERE have been, in spite of the seeming sameness, many approaches to Indian integration. There is the non-economic approach, which is not a complete approach, and there is the conservative approach, in which integration leads to monolithic nationhood, with the kind of simple process which made Sanskritization and westernization effective in the past. Neither history nor economics, neither language nor class can be ignored, and it is good that Indianness as broadly accepted allows for diversities of religion, community, tradition, mood and expression. It is only those elements which insist on the Indian nation being one in the sense of being single-stranded and not composite that are threatening the nation-building process and encouraging fascist trends. There are bound to be groups and communities within a nation and people can be simultaneously members of many different groups without being anti-national. Integration should not be strained to the point of denying the right to these diversities.

India is constitutionally a union which emphasizes the underlying unity, but the political, social and cultural structure is essentially federal in character. The talk of overriding the states is as unnecessary as the campaign against centralization. The balance has to be preserved, as it is in big countries like the Soviet Union and the United States or even in small countries like Britain. There is a solid south in all countries and the north–south polarization is not a special problem for India. The Confederate flag still flies in Atlanta and other places as a matter of sentiment but it is not a threat to American unity. The man from Arizona carries his local pride with him and has distaste for New England manners but they are all prepared to fight and die on the same battlefields for the same causes. The Uzbegs are Uzbegs more than Soviet citizens for certain purposes but are Soviet citizens above all for most purposes. Welshmen, Scotsmen, Englishmen have their separate cultural characteristics, but they are all British, in spite of the talk of Scottish autonomy north of Berwick-on-Tweed. India, with such a long history, with so many cultural inheritances, cannot be less composite, but this compositeness cannot be allowed to endanger political unity and territorial integrity.

Indian nation building does not seek the stimulus of external threat and wants to avoid the crucifying experience of a conflict like the American Civil War. The conflicts between languages, between regions, between communities would be mere irritations and abrasions of the integration process if economic sense and secular temper were to prevail. There is no need for pessimism, though mistakes have been made. If the several recommendations of the States Reorganization Commission, meant to emphasize the underlying unity of the country, had been accepted along with its recommendations for reorganization, many troubles could have been avoided. The opposition came from unenlightened people in the states, and even now there is some unenlightenment both in the north and south about language and about script. Education is a vital means of the long-term process and the rights of linguistic minorities are to be safeguarded. The present discussion on integration has resulted in many good forgotten recommendations, like the creation of more all-India services. Any integration, or education for it, can be only as a part of the social and economic revolution.

Hinduism and Islam, with not only their religious but social differentiation, are the two major strains in the make-up of the Indian nation. The coming of Islam made a difference to Indian history and nearly one thousand years of history cannot be erased. Islam did not conquer or convert all the people; Hinduism, in spite of social decay, had vitality and large parts of the country were beyond the influence of Islam. Three hundred years after the first battle of Panipat, it was clear that the two major communities were coming together and were, in spite of change of dynasty, becoming parts of the same social evolution, praying in temple or mosque. Neither religion could remain uninfluenced, though the orthodox tradition was maintained by Hindu and Muslim divines. It would not be correct to simplify the processes at work by saying that Akbar worked for unity or that Aurangzeb destroyed it. The processes of unification were interrupted by foreign interferences, and while two hundred years of British rule left its impress, the British regime by its policies contributed to the mutilation of the very unity for which it could take credit. The nationalist movement had its fractionalism and the upheaval of Gandhi had its reaction in the upheaval which Jinnah caused. The leaders of the majority community made mistakes ; when they could be generous, they were niggardly. The leaders of the minority community too made mistakes ; when they could be rightly insistent, they were irrational.

Constitutionally, Pakistan resulted from the secession of some parts of the country, though on the basis of religion. Most Hindus were aghast at such truncation, but not wholly for unselfish reasons ; most Indian Muslims were to realize that it did not do them good. Nevertheless, it has been accepted that India should not wish for the undoing of Pakistan and that Pakistan, though an Islamic state and consisting predominantly of Muslims, should not take extra-territorial interest in Indian Muslims. In Kashmir, contiguity operated in favour of both India and Pakistan. The leaders of Pakistan thought that Kashmir should be theirs because it was predominantly Muslim ; the leaders of India thought that because of accession, Kashmir was Indian and that its Muslim predominance did not make any difference. In Kashmir, India rebutted the two-nation theory. The crisis of extra-territorial loyalties arose in 1950 over the fate of the minority community in East Pakistan. There should be no discrimination and no genocide, but there can be no peace between the two countries if they take interest in the minority community in each other's territories. There is now another country with sovereign status, and it has a right to go its way. Norway and Sweden had been one country, and so had been Belgium and the Netherlands.

No one now wants religion to be banned, not even in communist countries. But there is recognition even among the sacerdotal classes in India that, while religion in the sense of respect for God and fellow beings should govern all activity, it should be relegated to its proper place. It should not be a differentiating factor in the exercise of political or civil rights. The greatest agencies of secularism are economic. The communal and caste conflicts are a part of the frustrations of an underdeveloped economy. When the people are drawn increasingly into the production processes, communities will cease to think of themselves as communities. There will have to be a common civil code as there is now a common criminal code. The most creative process of the present is the economic process. And, whatever might be the troubled processes, a nation has been in the making.

8. *Parliamentary Democracy*

PARLIAMENTARY democracy has acquired many complex procedures, largely derived from Britain, and people forget that it is only a refined form of democracy. Any democracy, whether Athenian or Indian, means government by discussion, by counting of heads, to oversimplify it, instead of by breaking of heads. Heads are broken and tyrannies arise if the people do not develop the atmosphere for discussion and the talent and the temper for it. The gigantic American democracy, which is a gargantuan process with complex patterns of public opinion, is sustained by the infinite capacity of the people for talk, for argument, and for debate. In the far different Soviet system too, the democratic processes depend on the capacity for debate, and as long as there is debate, the processes are bound to be democratic. Mensheviks and Bolsheviks battled against each other with talk; Stalin, whatever might have been his foxy statecraft, rose to power by his capacity to hold his own in discussion; and if Khrushchev was dominant, it is because he could out-talk most others. The democratic centralism of the communist apparatus depends as much on exchange of views as on manipulation.

Parliamentary democracy allows the maximum possible freedom for the largest number of people and their representatives to debate questions and arrive at decisions. It is a slow process. With more than one party, the artistry of parliamentary democracy lies in the agreed game of the opposition allowing the government to govern and the government allowing the opposition to oppose. In Britain the leader of Her Majesty's Opposition is as much honoured as the leader of Her Majesty's Government; at ceremonial functions, they sit side by side. In Parliament they respect each other, for today's leader of the opposition may be tomorrow's leader of the Government and today's shadow cabinet may be tomorrow's cabinet. As in Britain, there is in India direct representative democracy at the top. There can be no going back on adult suffrage, though it has multiplied the vagaries of parliamentary democracy, which has to be modified, if what Morley called the application of the fur coat to tropical conditions is not to be an unpractical operation. In Britain local self-government is the base on which parliamentary government rests. In India self-government at the village level is being established as the base.

The experiment of guided democracy or basic democracy has been shown to be either nearer to dictatorship than to democracy or more imperfect than parliamentary democracy. The presidential system, a fashion in Latin America, has grave uncertainties; it deprives the people of ultimate initiative and gives no guarantee of a succession of good leadership. The alternatives of indirect elections, rule by committees, referendum and recall have all only emphasized that politics is the art of the possible. Those who despair of parliamentary democracy working well in Indian conditions are thinking too literally of May's *Parliamentary Practice* and are bewildered by the fun that British commentators make of the archaic features of democracy in Britain. Indians do not possess the long British experience, but they have common sense, they know their interests, and they can discuss their problems. There are doubts about the capacity of parliamentary democracy to solve pressing economic problems immediately, but it only means that no democracy can. In the present pulls of power politics, the political parties run the danger of discrediting themselves so much that people may think of the rule of major-generals.

Parliamentary democracy is not a post-freedom development in India. From the time of Lord Cross's Act, right through the Minto–Morley and Montague–Chelmsford periods, the Indian people had experience of legislative work. The Gokhales had mature parliamentary temper; Motilal Nehru would have done credit to any opposition in any parliament. It was unfortunate that some good parliamentarians of the opposition parties were unseated in the last elections. A too pessimistic view of public life, however, might be an exaggerated view; the talk of political intrigue may have been overdone. The autobiographies of British statesmen show how intrigues become possible even among British political parties. When Lord John Russell wished to upset the Government, says Jennings, he did not move a resolution in the House of Commons; he held a private converse with a press lord and called a meeting at the Carlton Club. In India leaders of cabals and cliques call for special correspondents, inspire misleading stories and start signature campaigns. These and even Parnellite obstructionism and planned disturbances in legislatures may be passing phases. With the Congress maintaining its majorities throughout the country in three general elections, opposition parties do not feel they are alternative governments, but they are gaining confidence that the Congress can be defeated at least in some states to begin with. They have faith in the freedom and fairness of general elections, and it encourages faith in parliamentary democracy.

9. Battle of the Ballot

LORD MELBOURNE, when invited to become Prime Minister, thought it a damned bore and was in many minds. His private secretary protested: " Why, damn it; such a position never was occupied by any Greek or Roman, and, if it only last two months, it is well worth while to have been Prime Minister of England." " By God, that's true," replied Melbourne, " I'll go." Political ambition is not yet considered legitimate in India, though nobody is now impressed by the slogan of service. Political activitity may not lead to material benefits, apart from ministerial posts, but opportunities for gain will be open to those who have not achieved affluence in business or in their professions. Many, however, are driven by the demon of political conviction and passion, or attracted by the responsibilities of leadership, by the opportunity to make some history, by the ambition to contribute to legislation or to the treasures of eloquence. Membership of Parliament or the state legislatures means prestige and dignity, apart from opportunities, and while it may sometimes be a mere reward for superannuation, it has its prizes. The salary and allowances of a member or of a minister are not sufficient to make anyone wealthy, but he can feel that he can do some good, singly sometimes, collectively always.

India plunged into adult suffrage in conditions of mass illiteracy. This electorate has voted in three general elections and they have not only been free and fair but peaceful. The Indian voter may be illiterate, but he is supposed to know his interests. The electorates are large. The constituency for Parliament represents nearly a million people and the constituency for the state legislature anything from two to three lakh people. Election expenses cannot be met within the legal limits. In Britain most candidates of the

Conservative Party are expected to pay for their electoral organization and their election expenses, and the first question that is asked by a nominating committee is the amount which the candidate is able to pay. The system gives to the Conservative Party in Parliament a class bias far more emphatic than is warranted by its support in the country. If there are many men from Eton or Harrow, many retired army men or many company directors, it is not because they have special ability or want to form lobbies but because they come from the classes which can afford to nurse constituencies and win them for the Conservative Party. The Labour Party does not seek candidates who can pay organizational and election expenses. It increases its paying membership, raises funds by social activities, asks for special contributions and expects local trade unions and co-operative societies to make payments from their political funds. The sums required for Labour candidates are smaller because voluntary workers are available and the divisional party provides both organization and premises. Nevertheless, it is not easy to raise funds. The auditing of election expenses in Britain is strict, but Conservatives are not willing to disclose the contributions of companies to party funds and to accept the principle of shareholders' consent to the contributions.

Among Indian political parties, the main consideration in selecting candidates is not only their intellectual and moral calibre but their ability to secure success at the polls. The power of local appeal and, in the case of leading men, the power of personality would be an asset. As three or four constituencies for the state legislature make a constituency for Parliament, candidates for the state legislature can carry on their backs the candidate for Parliament and not unoften a strong candidate for Parliament can give a pull to the candidates for the state legislatures. The problem is to reduce the uncertainties and sort out and screen the candidates. In the large Indian constituencies, few candidates can afford to contribute fully to the organizational and election expenses ; the burden falls mainly on the party exchequer. It should then be possible to select as many candidates as possible on merit, but this does not happen usually and it is difficult to ensure utter impartiality in the Congress, in spite of clearly laid down rules, because of the greater temptations available in a party which has been in power for so long. Talent and resources are not enough; luck is also necessary and it is elusive. Ministers and leading members manage to get nomination for seats considered to be safe.

Election expenses are a crushing burden in India. The Congress has had an advantage because it has had larger resources, but not all Congress candidates can be sure of help on an individual basis. It is a hit-or-miss affair. Congress propaganda and appeal may help or not. All parties talk of limiting election expenses, but even legitimate expenses would be large enough in such large constituencies. Indian voters have not only to be convinced of a candidate's worth but be persuaded to go to the polling booth. The election law is strict, but direct elections on such dimensions are bound to be expensive. No party suggests indirect elections, and adult suffrage is a hazardous, grinding process. By a law, companies have been allowed to contribute to party funds with shareholders' consent, but this also gives the Congress the advantage, though the capitalist classes have begun to invest in any party which has a chance of success at the polls. Legislators are able to increase their salaries and allowances and they may have to contribute more to the party funds. Even then, unless parties are equally affluent, they cannot hope to fight elections on equal terms.

10. Direct Action

FOR a people striving for freedom, agitation is the breath of life, and when they become free, they find it difficult to stop agitating. The place of direct action in a democracy has often come up for half-hearted discussion in India. Democracy has meant parliamentary democracy as it is embodied in the Constitution, but there seems to be no equally approximate idea of direct action. How direct is direct action to be? It is assumed that with representative institutions and self-government at various levels there would be adequate scope for self-expression and for even energetic expression of political opposition. The right to expression and the right to assemble are fundamental rights, though all rights are subject to reasonable restrictions. The right to demonstrate, to take out processions, to withdraw from work are rights which are generally protected, and peaceful picketing, which is often not peaceful, has become a part of the right to strike. These forms of action cannot be confused with what is called direct action. Where violence is associated with any form of action, it is not only condemnable but punishable, and as Alexander Hamilton said, energy should not be confounded with violence.

Some Indian socialists maintain that direct action has a place in democracy; they probably do not mean anything more than that people have a right to refuse to pay taxes or not to co-operate with the Government in several ways. These abstract rights cannot be defined, protected or even discussed. Those who assert these rights have in mind the redressal of grievances, not the overthrow of governments, and when they think of action beyond the terms of the Constitution and the framework of representative institutions, they are relying upon Gandhi and his ideas of Satyagraha, not upon political theory and practice.

It is necessary to separate Gandhi's Satyagraha from direct action as it is sought to be enunciated and practised. Gandhi thought of a new form of action, based on his idea of non-violence, in the conditions of South Africa and gave the name " Satyagraha " to it. It means holding on to truth. As Gandhi practised it, it was something more than civil disobedience; it was moral aggression based on truth and non-violence. The aim was conversion, not coercion. It was after long years of practice of Satyagraha in various forms that Gandhi left behind a corpus of doctrine and practice. He was the author of Satyagraha and he was the best commentator on it. Even in his life time, it was shown that nobody else had a clear idea of Satyagraha or could practise it. Gandhi alone had the courage to withdraw Satyagraha whenever he felt it became tainted and he alone could ensure purity of means and ends. After his death, Satyagraha became distorted and took many ugly forms. His fasting, for which he had a rigid code of discipline, has been caricatured into hunger-strikes. It would be wrong to call him in support of what is said to be direct action. The rights of protest and non-co-operation, which are allowed under the law, must be distinguished from the kinds of action often adopted for redressal of specific grievances, and direct action for political aim cannot be approved by anyone who wants progress to be peaceful. The leaders of the agitation against the communist regime in Kerala in 1959 said that their aim was the overthrow of the Government when they need not have said so; in promoting direct action for the redressal of grievances, communists, socialists and others have in mind the undermining of the stability of the Government, though they do not say so, and their object would be overthrow of the Government, if that were possible.

The aim and the extent of action determine its character. In Britain strikes are legitimate but a general strike is illegal. The 1926 general strike showed that while the aim of a strike can be redressal of grievances, the aim of a general strike can be nothing but political. Its purpose need not be declared to be to overthrow the Government, but the effect of a successful general strike would be the overthrow of the Government in a country where it has been held that the only means of bringing down a Government is the loss of the confidence of the Commons in a division or of the people in a general election. There is no more scope for Wat Tylers or for repetition of the Gordon riots or of the militancy of the suffragette movement in Britain. The usual way of bringing a grievance to the notice of the public and the Government is to write a letter to *The Times* or some other newspaper ; the greatest revolutionary act in recent times was to try to run away with the Mace on the table of the House of Commons. In the United States, agitation took the form of filibustering or middle-of-the-road mugwumpism ; now Negro leaders have adopted Gandhian techniques. In India, walk-outs have been a form of parliamentary obstructionism, varied by processions to Parliament House. It is possible that with greater experience of parliamentary working there will be many polite forms of protest which will make political action indirect and constitutional rather than direct and unconstitutional.

11. A Government of Laws

THE republican citizens of India enjoy common citizenship, but every citizen has yet to feel that he is subject to common laws and that the Government is a government of laws and not merely of men. The backwoodsmen of America did not know they were Americans, in their pioneering days in the west, and were conscious of being citizens only when they were made to submit to the operation of law. The American nation was, in fact, made only in the terrible experience of the Civil War, which was a test of common citizenship. Abraham Lincoln fought indirectly for equal rights for Negroes, but directly for the oneness of the union and the supremacy of the constitution. In due course, every American, whether belonging to the unionist camp or the confederate camp, whether democrat or republican, felt the force of law, took recourse to the courts for definable wrongs and invoked the Supreme Court with faith in its impartiality and sense of justice. Whatever their racial extraction and whatever their stage of development, the people knew they were Americans, above everything, not just New Englanders, New Mexicans or Texans. The Soviet Union is an example of a state based on different nationalities but bound together by strong central authority. The one-party system in the Soviet Union operates powerfully and party is a part of the Soviet Constitution. In communist countries there may seem to be no rule of law, according to the Anglo-Saxon concept, but no state can exist without law and communist states have their own legal systems.

The educated Indian is legal minded, though he does not exert himself to exercise his rights for civil wrong, and the uneducated Indian is easily drawn into litigation for property rights. In recent years personal freedom has become a source of litigation, and there is no end to writ petitions in the High Courts.

If the rule of law is to be paramount, the people must know what it means. Even in Britain, the rule of law became real only when a large part of the population consisting of the working class became organized. In Indian conditions illiteracy imposes great limitations. Even for the educated, it has become impossible to follow the enormous mass of legislation which has become necessary for a welfare state. The legal system can be simplified only if the social and economic system is simplified. If people do not know the laws that govern them, they cannot assert their rights or discharge their duties under them. Fundamental Rights are the most popular part of the Indian Constitution but even they are little known. The rule of law means more than anything else equality before the law without distinction between persons and the operation of law under a country-wide system. If there are no distinctions, people must be able to assert and exercise their rights freely. As long as the people remain largely inert and do not develop the constitutional and legal sense, they are poor republicans and poor citizens.

In any political system and under any constitution, equality before the law would be a myth without economic equality. Nobody is in a position to assert his rights unless he has achieved sufficient economic means. Even if he has the economic means and the courage, he cannot fight alone; he must seek the help of other individuals fighting for the same or similar causes. Before trade unionism became widespread and a civil and political force, individual liberty was proving to be unreal. The Indian citizen is not among the most fortunately placed people on earth. He does not know the laws which govern his life and he is not sufficiently organized; and he has to safeguard his rights not only against the Government but against other men. There is little correspondence between the people and the administration, and as the party system develops, the machinery of government may lose the popular touch. In a federal state, where the constituent elements are a check on each other, pluralism is unavoidable. It will be more complex than an absolutist or monolithic state and will require understanding of its complex working.

There is faith in litigation and in the judiciary. The majesty of justice is upheld not only in other ways but in the solid brick and mortar of the highest courts and the High Courts and the Supreme Court in India have imposing exteriors. They house a long tradition. But justice is costly and involves frustrating delays. There have been also no startling developments in Indian jurisprudence. There is yet no Indian jurisprudence at all. It is the joint task of the bar and the bench, and while both are suffering a diminution in stature, leading members of the bar are not easily attracted to the bench. The Indian pioneers of the Madras High Court bench came from the lower ranks of the *mofussil* courts. Yet Muthuswami Aiyar who acted as Chief Justice could write succinct judgments in excellent English. Bashyam Iyengar, who could not speak eloquently in English, could expound judicial principles with originality and expertness. There was legal genius at work in Bengal and in Bombay, too. The Allahabad High Court produced a great jurist in Syed Mahumud. In the general despondency over the fall of standards of English, the present fall in the standard of judgments is forgotten.

The character of litigation has been changing in a country which is legislating itself into socialism. There are no longer fat landlords who pay rich retainers to lawyers who could contribute royalty to some cause. Lawyers have to work at more briefs than before to earn well, though Company Law has become as rich a source of income as Hindu Law and the Transfer of Property Act were before. In criminal law, Bufuz and his latter-day versions like Birkenhead are rare ; arguments and recourse to the right of appeal have become more useful than examination and cross-examination even in sensational fraud cases. If some talk disparagingly of writ petitions, it is not because they misunderstand the spirit of the Constitution but because they would like less of litigation. A mixed economy like India's, with the ever-increasing omnipotence of the state and with a strong attachment to the legal tradition, still means for many what Voltaire meant when he said that he had been ruined twice, once when he gained a suit and once when he lost a suit. This cannot be helped, for every law has a loophole, especially when it is loosely drafted, and there are too many bad draftsmen in the legal departments. The most fruitful source of the new litigation naturally is the Constitution, though there is yet no constitutional sense, worthy of the Constitution.

No Indian jurisprudence will emerge for some time, though three High Courts have celebrated their centenaries and there is much talk of the traditions of the bar and the bench. There is yet little organization and research. Law colleges are just passages to the profession. Without denying the soundness of other systems, Indians may like to deviate a little from the present adherence to a too rigid system of Anglo-Saxon jurisprudence. As American usage is different from English usage, an American jurisprudence has emerged. Whatever their distortions in a one-party regime, communist countries have developed their own system of jurisprudence, and it may not be wrong to say that they have less of law and more of justice. There can be too much law and not much justice in countries which can be called democratic.

12. Conservatives Fight Back

INDIAN conservatism is so well entrenched that it needs no party to defend it, but so many parties profess to be progressive or socialist that there is a conservative party. The Swatantra Party is supported by businessmen, big and small, ex-rulers, rich peasants and anti-communists, but it has an irremovable base as old as Adam Smith. Mr. Rajagopalachari, the real leader of the party, said that if there was no opposition in a parliamentary democracy, it would be necessary to invent one, and in asking for a conservative opposition, he is both a pragmatist and a political scientist. He is the imaginative and inventive Indian Abbé de Sieyes. For nearly forty years he has been in a kind of opposition, though he was the last Governor-General of India. When he was in the Union Government, as Home Minister, he was inclined to be authoritarian and put all his moral prescriptions in the now dead Press Act. The freedom which he used indefatigably as a free thinker is invaluable to a people who deserve gadflies as much as they deserve godfathers, and his conservatism should cause no surprise, for he always thought like a Tory, even when he talked like a radical. It is not worse at any rate to speak for those who are conservative and rich than to speak for those who are radical and rich. When great questions end, little parties begin.

It is now fashionable to caricature congressmen. " Mamma," asked a Whig child, " are Tories born wicked or do they grow wicked ? " " They are born wicked and grow worse," said Mamma. Mr. Rajagopalachari has developed similar dislike of the Congress and its hectic policies of what seem to be constant shift and change, and to him Congress socialism is not, as Mencken described socialism, simply the degenerate capitalism of bankrupt capitalists but red ruin. Nor is Mr. Rajagopalachari like the first British Tories, who in the Irish language meant plunderers, interested in preserving Anglicanism and squirearchy. It is a misfortune of the Congress that he has rarely agreed with it, though he was one of the most eminent congressmen and was close to Gandhi. It is, however, a mark of courage for anyone as progressive-minded as Mr. Rajagopalachari to work for a conservative party, though Disraeli, in his early days, called a Conservative government an organized hypocrisy. Mr. Rajagopalachari is working for an opposition, not for a government, organized or unorganized. Whenever he propounds a conundrum, he thinks he has made an epigram, like Arthur Balfour, but his epigrams are widely appreciated.

It is Indian Bloomsbury which provides the intellectual base for a conservative party, which will be run and managed by privileged interests. The party, which results from a combination of intellectual celerity and profiteering instinct, may be redundant in the conditions of the country and an anachronism with adult suffrage. But it has reason to exist, if it causes rethinking and at least among what is called parties on the right, it is a secular party which believes in argument, not in direct action. It is thus promoting respect for constitutionalism. The Tories who became Conservatives in Britain claimed that they were conservative because the Whigs were subversive. Those who like Mr. Rajagopalachari worked for freedom and now refuse to face its consequences could not have had an idea of the content of freedom ; they seek to resist the corrosion of change which is inevitable in establishing new economic and social relationship. Mr. Rajagopalachari thinks that the parties which claim to be working for socialism are merely working for positions of power, but if he understood power in the economic and social sense, the meaning of so many parties working for socialism is that the total situation of the country has a significance which many parties are eager to grasp. A conservative party, by whatever name it is called, is bound to reflect those interests which, howsoever rightly critical of measures of legislation or of administrative action, will be pitted against change and progress. It is difficult to think that Mr. Rajagopalachari will be for ever a party to the entrenchment of interests amidst privileged surroundings. He is, however, a bulwark of constitutional progress because he opposes everything constitutionally. That is partly because he has never had his heart in Satyagraha and partly because the ex-rulers behind him will not agree to parade and demonstrate.

13. Socialism in Theory and Practice

THERE is something like Indian socialism. It is not because it is a revealed text or an adopted doctrine, but because anything that grows in the Indian soil cannot but be Indian. The only socialism which has inspired hope and fear in mankind is scientific socialism, which began with Marx and soon became international in inspiration and scope. In a big country, national tradition is bound to have an impact on the internationalism to which people like Trotsky clung fatalistically. The absolutism of the Romanoffs in Russia could not be discarded like a winter cloak; the Czars fought for security from the Baltic to the Black Sea, and so did Stalin. The Manchus and Confucius are deeply embedded in the fatherhood of Chairman Mao. Even in smaller countries, history has its hang-overs, though the communism of the smaller countries has the character of a carbon copy. The separation of socialism and communism began with Lenin's hectic calumnies against the social democrats, and socialists and communists have since then followed their separate courses. Both have derived inspiration from Marx and both have been internationalist, but they have had their separate internationals. The communists have had the advantage of a base in the Soviet Union, and this has made much difference to the fearful aspects of communism and its conflict with socialism. But even the Soviet Union has been changing under the impact of its economy and the pressure of international forces, and, therefore, communism has begun to change.

The association of socialism and communism as some kind of Siamese twins is still as popular among conservatives as their divergences are among communists and socialists. Apart from the definitions given in dictionaries and the popular but not scientific description that socialism will ensure social security to each according to work and communism to each according to needs, socialism and communism have identical aims about ownership, income and planning. The differences which have developed suggest that they are differences only over tactics. Only communist parties, however, have been able to bring about socialist transformation, with the help of war and Soviet help, and not socialist parties. There have been other equally important differences. The socialists have grown to value democracy, while the communists with Leninism for guidance and the Soviet Union as their base have believed in a rigid application of dictatorship of the proletariat, which has degenerated in practice into dictatorship of the party and gradually of the central committee. As the means have influenced the ends, socialism has become different from communism. The ideas have been simple but the ideologies have become complex, and sometimes it is like a Marx Brothers' version of Marx.

Indian socialists began as students of Marxism and admirers of the Russian Revolution. They were more in sympathy with Lenin's shock tactics than with the metaphysics which seemed to be a part of the revolution which developed into Gandhi's leadership. He was Indian in his whole being and they were not, and Jawaharlal Nehru alone understood his genius and found that he alone had a plan of action. The Congress socialists, who were not the original Indian socialists, wanted to convert the nationalist revolution into a socialist revolution, but they did not know how to set about it and became a sect of scholastic socialists. They had neither the patience nor the capacity for revolution ; they became too ambitious and too ambivalent. The result was an ineffectual type of socialism. The evolution of the Congress, disappointing for doctrinal purposes, has been more natural and has had the impetus of inevitability making it more Indian than alien. This has been largely Jawaharlal Nehru's work. If theory and practice should go together for assured socialist transformation, socialism is safer in the hands of those who can protect and implement it.

The search for Indianness has been a desperate struggle for communism. Mr. Louis Fischer and others, who have sought to pit Gandhi and Stalin against each other, have been as cruel to Gandhi and Stalin as Dange and others were in earlier years when they pitted Lenin and Gandhi against each other. The attempt to escape from Marxism, for avoiding the tortuous courses of Leninism, has led to much unscientific socialism. Utopian socialism led to genetics ; what is known as Vedantic socialism, or socialism derived from the *Upanisheds*, has meant revivalism. Those who made a socialism of Gandhi's economic ideas found that it was only compatible with an India consisting of a small population without industrialization and in a state of anarchy or co-operative commonness. Mr. Roy's cerebration resulted in Royism ; others' cerebration led to nothing. Socialism would be simple, if it were not to serve a society as complex as that of the industrial age, and it gives rise to concepts varying from centralism to statelessness. The variations in practice have become many, and it is possible to trace them all the way from United States capitalism to Soviet collectivism.

Sir William Harcourt said in the last years of Victoria's reign : " We are all socialists now " ; it became a fashionable joke. The Swatantra Party seeks to say : " We are all conservatives now " ; it is also a joke, though not yet fashionable. The conditions of an underdeveloped economy, the technological revolution all round, the tremendous urges of the people for better standards of living and equality make socialism inescapable. Capitalism is out of date in Indian conditions, though socialism presents as many problems as communism. Marxism has been muted in Soviet experience and is largely misunderstood, though it helps economic understanding. There is both alien, or international, and Indian inspiration. A vast country like India with a long tradition cannot be imitative even in its socialism and follow what some Cominform decides. Indian conditions also impose the democratic process. The peasant predominates and, without feudal conditions, he is not malleable material, as he was in China. Even the growing proletariat will not be too responsive to total control. The task of socialist leadership is to face the facts, interpret social and economic forces correctly and guide them. Schisms will wither and the unity of socialist forces become real, if it is understood that power lies ultimately with the people.

Socialism, which is known to be authoritarian, though not absolutist, collectivist in tendency, ethical in motive, religious and philosophical in its sources, realistic, empiricist, total, integral and, as long as the world consists of sovereign states, nationalist, cannot be simplified in the modern state, though it leads to simpler social and economic structures. The schism in internal communism has shown how nationalist are communist states and how they make theories of national interests. Communism's lesson that the democratic process is worth preserving wherever it is possible has been sufficiently reinforced, but democratic socialism, which in communist countries has been politically a self-contradictory term, has little hope to offer elsewhere if it ceases to be socialism.

14. Planning: Illusion and Reality

IN A planned economy, the planning set-up attracts most attention, and even statistics come only next. Who is planning? The Indian Planning Commission is the central body for planning and there are no planning boards or even planning departments in the states. The planners are supposed to be thinkers at large, and half of them are important members of the Central Government, with little time to plan or think. The other half of the planners, who could be wholetime thinkers, have hardly more time to think. They are not like the Princeton thinkers who are left free for advanced study. Almost every day there are documents to be studied and discussed, and the discussions which are to be carried on with visiting experts and dignitaries can be exhausting. One plan leads to another and many plans ahead are planned in outline in what is known as perspective planning; the Planning Commission is throughout busy estimating the progress of one plan and projecting the next.

On one condition only can planners be free to plan as they like, and that is by having nothing to do with the execution of the plans. This is still suggested by some who want planning to be thinking and nothing more. In their view, the Planning Commission could be a subordinate or subsidiary body of experts, who would make recommendations for the Government to accept or reject, and need not be an integral part of the Government. The suggested implication is that a planning set-up of the present kind would lead to totalitarian tendencies and subordination of policy and measures to a rigid system of recommendations and doctrine. Less polite people have called the Planning Commission a super cabinet. Yet, many are not satisfied with the present set-up because it is not rigid enough. Jawaharlal Nehru, who was responsible for the idea and the apparatus of planning, had begun his association with planning, when he became chairman of the National Planning Committee set up by the Congress before the war. The committee and its too many subcommittees did much compilation and some thinking, but the many volumes of principles and programmes, which were produced on behalf of the committee, show that planning, divorced from responsibility and action, would be largely platonic.

There is nothing wrong, at the impersonal level, with the Planning Commission and the planning set-up, but everything is not necessarily right with planning because of it. India can draw upon the experiences of several countries, especially the Soviet Union. But as only communist countries have had planned economies, it has meant that either planning is totalitarian in concept and content or that only communist countries can plan successfully. Now even non-communist countries have planned economies. In Britain both Conservatives and Labour plan, though differently. India's problem is to stick to processes known to be democratic and to constitutional ways, and plan for turning an underdeveloped economy into a self-generating economy. The lesson from communist countries has been that underdeveloped countries can make rapid technological advances by planning and sacrificing, at least in the short term, the democratic processes and many consumer needs. Such planning is not easily accepted in India where socialism, even to many socialists, means only social and economic equality of some kind. For those who want to lead the largely inert people into participation in planned economic processes, people's planning has been a suitable catchphrase. Not many people can plan or think, though most of them know their needs. If these needs alone were taken into account, economic policies might mean a welfare state or a capitalist state depending on the profit motive but not a socialist or even a rapidly developing state. The rate of development is important for an underdeveloped people, but it would mean a high rate of investment. The people would not save and invest, unless the aims are clear and ambitious enough.

It was said that the Second Plan was to be the result of planning from below, and the Third Plan also was to be a people's plan. But nowhere were the people drawn into discussion. The state plans had as little of people's planning in them as the overall plan. Nowhere do the people plan; somebody plans for them, whether in Etawah or Alma Ata. It is only then possible to fix priorities and plan intelligently. The people come in very much when resources, especially manpower resources, are to be mobilized, and large-scale co-operation is wanted. It is the people that have to contribute the financial resources, too, and no people will want planning unless they know what it is and why they should make any sacrifices for it. Unfortunately, neither the Congress nor any other political party has been able to take planning to the people or the people to planning.

It should be possible to take planning to the people, even if they cannot be consulted in planning. For participation in planning, one should know one's share of the plan. The national income, the *per capita* income, and such formulas mean little to the people. Nor will mere bread or cloth, even at a reasonable price, mean planning to them. To comprehend the plan, especially the production figures, they must know their share in the production process. Each state plan has to be broken down into small bits, not according to development blocks but according to factories and fields. Each production unit should know its target and the means by which it is sought to be achieved and each member of the unit should know his contribution. Publicity must come from within the plan. Every Indian should be able to know what he is in the plan. Then will questions be asked. If one is to do his bit for the plan, what will one get in return? Thus planning and publicity will be one process. This is not totalitarianism; it is common sense.

15. Three Plans

INDIA'S First Plan was not much of a plan; it took over several old projects and integrated them into a scheme of economic and social development. Its emphasis was on agriculture, irrigation, power and transport. But it was a substantial contribution to the principles of planning. The Second Plan carried the basic policies further and aimed at a larger increase in investment, production and employment. Its emphasis on heavy industries, its assignment of a key role to the public sector and its provision of three steel plants pleased the more ardent advocates of planning. Socialist planning was projected for the first time. The total investment, public and private, per annum had at the beginning of the First Plan been Rs. 500 crores; at its end it reached Rs. 850 crores. At the end of the Second Plan, the level was of about Rs. 1600 crores. In agriculture the average level of production of foodgrains went up from 50 million tons in 1950–1 to 78 million tons in 1960–1; the yield per acre also rose significantly. The progress of industrial production was more spectacular in the ten years. All this was not enough.

India's 450 million form one-sixth of the world's population. The land area is the seventh largest; of the 721 million acres, one-fifth is under forest and two-fifths under cultivation. Only about 20 per cent of the cultivated area is under irrigation, and in the struggle to be independent of the variable monsoon rains, irrigation is important. India has large reserves of high quality iron ore, 50 billion tons of coal, and new oil fields are being discovered. Abundant monazite sands provide the basic sources of atomic energy. There is endless electric potential in the river waters. But the population keeps growing at the rate of 2·5 per cent per year, and about seven-ninths of the people are in the 570,000 villages. Among the towns, barely above a hundred have a population of more than 100,000 each ; seven cities have a population of more than a million each. Seventy per cent of the working population, about 130 million, are engaged in agriculture, which contributes nearly half the national income, and by 1975 the working population may increase to 250 million. Planning must be ambitious enough. The achievements have been substantial, but there is much more to be achieved, a higher rate of savings, a higher rate of investment, and a higher rate of development.

The Third Plan aimed at an increase in national income of over 5 per cent per annum, self-sufficiency in foodgrains, expansion of basic industries, greater use of manpower resources and greater equality of opportunities and reduction in disparities. There was hope of reaching the stage of self-sustained growth in the next two or three plan periods, when the national income would go up by about 30 per cent and *per capita* income by about 17 per cent. The effort for financial resources for the Third Plan, with an investment of Rs. 8000 crores in the public sector and Rs. 4100 crores in the private sector, had to be big. There has, however, been reluctance, especially in the states, to raise the additional taxation required. Foreign assistance is an uncertain factor and the balance of trade will remain uneven, till the developed countries feel they can be generous. With so much outlay, a large part of the physical targets at least could be achieved. There has been waste and extravagance, but much of the investment filters through. After three years of the plan, however, industrial targets have not been achieved and the failure in agriculture is disheartening.

A plan is not a list of projects or a balance-sheet of resources. It is a blueprint for the allocation of all the resources available to the community for different uses. The process is complex and there are many stresses and strains. The administration is not equal to the task and the people have not been sufficiently mobilized, mainly because of party politics. Yet, everyone is agreed that without planning, there can be no progress. The plans have been an experience and many lessons have been learnt. There is much expertise now, and the Fourth Plan, with its tentative target of a Rs. 20,000 crore investment, pushes the perspective forward.

The take-off stage will still be not near and there are uncertain elements. There is no certainty how far planning should be rigid or flexible. By implication, planning in Indian conditions meant socialism, though it has come to be only slowly accepted. Divorce between planning and socialist thinking would be incongruous, but a mixed economy offers mixed incentives, and deficit financing, without controls, leads to inflation. Every part of the community is discontented. Whether about the salary scales of government employees, the wages of labour, the allocation of planning priorities, the price and supply mechanism, thinking has yet to be integrated.

There are contradictory conditions. Where production is socialist, the distributive system is still capitalist ; where distribution is socialist or state-controlled, the production processes are capitalist. Rent control is socialist but land remains a capitalist commodity. These inner contradictions within the bigger contradictions have caused confusion and without Jawaharlal Nehru and his strident pronouncements, the suspicion is spreading that, in spite of socialist professions, the Government are capitalist-minded, or that, in spite of what is professed, central ministers, state ministers, and the whole apparatus of administration are not only rooted in the past but are trustees for the capitalist class. There are bound to be shortcomings in a party and in an administration which have to meet the needs of a social and economic system which must change before they also can change. Some contradictions can be removed. The public corporations which are being set up in increasing numbers are not run as institutions of socialism. In the public sector, the contract system vitiates the atmosphere with its corruption. Elementary and secondary education has a semi-feudal set-up. Planning has to be at least national in aims and execution.

16. Padding and Puddering

INDIA'S First Plan ran to 668 pages and the Second Plan to 641 shorter, more closely printed, pages. The two plans had to explain much, but the "approach" and the "objectives" were stated in too many words. The Third Plan did not carry such a heavy load of general, and often misty, statement; with 400 pages, it set a standard of slimness. It could not be reduced to a mere list of items appended to an outline of the plan. For whom are the documents known as "plans" meant? For the planners, for the central and state governments, for those who execute the plans, and for the people. The plan is not one document; those who have to carry out the programme cannot find everything in it. But the plan is of interest to all people and it should be readable, which would mean that it should be clear, concise, short and possess style. The reports produced by Indian commissions and committees are heavy, prolix and long, but it should be possible even for Indians to produce intelligible reports. It is not composition that makes a good report; the mind behind it is important. As Samuel Butler said: "It takes two to say a thing—a sayee as well as a sayer, and the one is as essential to any true saying as the other."

There is much that is excisable in the first three plans, and what could be excised is "puddering", a word adopted from Shakespeare by Ivor Brown to describe "jargantuan" combinations of words, the meaning of which is not clear, or what Mr. Polly of H. G. Wells called "sesquippledan verboojuice". There can be no clear expression without clear thinking, which is hard work, and Indian planning is largely a lazy process. Neither style nor "Saxon English" is what is required. The simple rule is to choose the familiar word and the precise word and avoid the superfluous word. Fowler and Gowers have warned against verbosity in adjectives and adverbs, which makes every crisis acute and every emergency grave. The vagueness of adjectives like " considerable ", " appreciable ", " substantial ", the verbosity of prepositions like " as regards ", " as to ", " in connection with ", " in regard to ", the volubility of adverbial phrases containing words like " case ", " instance ", " aspect ", " point of view ", " viewpoint ", the indirectness of auxiliary verbs like " is not prepared to ", " is not in a position to ", " does not see his way to ", prove irresistible. Churchill, in a memorandum entitled *Brevity*, issued in 1940, wanted departments to put an end to padding : " Let us not shrink from using the short expressive phrase even it it is conversational." The Indian planners want to be polite and to avoid crude statements, but they have been guilty of padding. Jargon, overworked metaphors like " background ", " backlog ", " blueprint ", " bottleneck "—with absurdities like " the biggest bottleneck in housing,", " bottlenecks must be ironed out ", " what is planned is actually a series of bottlenecks "—" breakdown ", " ceiling ", " repercussion ", " target ", seductive words like " achieve ", " anticipate ", " envisage ", " implement ", " materialize ", " utilize ", " minimum ", " visualize ", " involve ", abstract words, clichés, and words like " position " and " situation ", when loosely used, do not help understanding.

There was much puddering and verbosity in all the plans. Vague words like " aspect ", " perspective ", " comprehensive ", " incorporate ", " evoke ", " current ", " accelerate ", are vaguely or wrongly used and a few pages are thus wasted. Vague phrases like " various levels ", " all levels ", " levels of expenditure ", or " central objective ", " broad objective ", and " essential objective " and expletives like " finally " are extensively used ; a few pages could have been gained by avoiding them. There could be much saving of space if stock phrases—" it is now estimated ", " it was felt ", " it may be stated ", " it is no exaggeration to say ", " it need hardly be stressed ", " in other words "—and clumsy statements like " regarding population growth, only a few observations seem necessary " or " the overall results of the Third Plan may be stated briefly ", could be avoided; it is enough to make the " observations " or state the " results". There are more ludicrous examples.

> Development is a continuous process; it touches all aspects of community life and has to be viewed comprehensively.
>
> Within this broad approach, the Second Five Year Plan has been formulated with reference to the following principal objectives.
>
> It must be stressed that reduction in inequalities in income and wealth can follow only from the totality of measures and instrumental changes undertaken as a part of the plan.
>
> Mention may be made finally of the fact that the yield from estate duty has so far been negligible.
>
> The foregoing observations are not meant to indicate that any or all of the measures mentioned can be adopted immediately.

No planning can be effective, if it has to be explained so confusedly. Indian planning is probably not effective because the planning is in English.

17. Village Community

IN INDIAN villages, cactus keeps spreading in clusters beyond broken hedges into the wall-less homes built of mud. The scene symbolizes the endless trance and endless vigil of a people who have slumbered for centuries and become a part of the environment of slush and dirt and disease. To the upper crust of the caste-ridden village society, the plough is the symbol of life and harvests bring festival atmosphere; there is the hard lower crust of people to whom life and death are not different, and they constitute most of what are callously called the millions. Sometimes the rains do not come and there is drought, followed by famine conditions; at other times there is too much rain and whole villages are washed away. The cactus continues to spread, encircling the villages with its prickly grip. Not all the six lakh villages are now under the old spell, which Hindu or Muslim rulers did not break. With freedom, there were whisperings of change, and it was felt that to sleep-walk is not to live. This revolution in the mind is not known to the new community leaders who seem to come from another world. The village folk no longer listen to old wives' tales; they question, grumble, and ask for everything that the world can give. This is called the revolution of rising expectations.

The revolution has been going on, unrecognized by people in the towns. The villages are not content to provide the manure for urbanization. The towns have roads and water taps, though the dairy man, the vegetable seller, the sweeper, and the scavenger who slave for others belong to a world of submerged fury. The unorganized urban labour finds its recruits in the village, where there are too many who have to live on too little land, and there is a link between rural needs and urban needs. Beneath is a cavernous underground, of the lava and brimstone of raw emotions, dark, lustreless elements. Revolutions are silent and devour their children silently, till they are forced to be violent.

There were two parallel movements to resurrect Indian villages, the agrarian agitation organized by the Congress and the tenancy reforms which the British Government introduced in spurts of reforming zeal. In some states, peasant proprietorships had been recognized by enlightened British rulers ; in other states, land had been indiscriminately farmed out among middle men, who developed into a baronial class competing with the ruling princes for influence, privilege and power. In states like Uttar Pradesh, agrarian revolution seemed possible, with more than two million landlords, some of them with only small slices of land. With freedom, landlordism was abolished painlessly, which meant compensation in cash and in bonds. This was a burden which communist countries could do without, but India was working under a constitution which provided for compensation, though by amendment the amount of compensation was left to the legislatures. The difference between expropriation with compensation and expropriation without compensation has made a difference to the pace of land reform. In India all the tenants freed from landlordism could not be made owners of land in one stage ; in some states, they had to pay for ownership, a kind of contribution to the compensation funds. Landlords, who were deprived of their income as middle men, could keep some land of their own and some properties on it, and the smaller among them who were landlords only in name were given rehabilitation grants to be saved from pauperization.

The freed peasants had to deal with too many authorities, instead of the old landlords, who were exacting but could be identified. Instead of the oppressiveness of the middle man, there was new insecurity, with no end to land reform or to talk of it. Land reform is the most difficult of reforms to implement, and with even the promised land reforms not taking effect, the small peasant with an uneconomic holding has a hard and difficult life. The landless, whose number is large, do not find enough employment. To apply the classification which is fashionable in socialist countries, the rich peasant and the middle peasant alone can get on. The Congress is dominated by rich peasants and land reform is, therefore, said to be tardy and unreal. There were to be ceilings on land, but there is no legislation yet for it throughout the country, and where there is legislation, ceilings are too high or too unreal. There was to be a drive for co-operative farming, but only rich peasants have the initiative to form co-operatives and manage to get fat government loans. Irrigation has been extended but irrigation rates are high and scare away the small peasant. Land is to belong to the tiller, but many who do not take interest in cultivation are allowed to own land. Agricultural production has increased but not at the rate at which the country needs it. There is endless talk of helping the peasant, but it is only now that incentives are being offered to him, and most of the incentives are good intentions which do not reach him.

The Indian village has roused much romanticism and inspired much bucolic poetry. Any further idealization of the villages as scenes of pastoral peace with aged cows treated as sacred is recognized to be unhelpful. There was much hope when the movement for what is known as community development was started on a large scale under state auspices. It aimed at total transformation. The village community was to be organized for new life, with health centres, recreation facilities, sales depots and agriculture was to be supplemented with revived or newly established village industries. The results have been confined only to some villages. Roadside villages with good communications, villages which can sell their produce easily to towns, villages which have been electrified and villages which have produced leadership or in which the legislators of the district have taken interest, have gone ahead; they have industries, schools, health centres. But there are villages in the interior which are worse than they were thirty or forty years ago. Communications are the first need; electricity has a revolutionary impact. There has been as much confusion in theory as in practice, and there is no end to the compartmentalization of economic problems into rural economics, growth economics, labour economics, industrial economics and so on.

The reorganization of life in the village had to be based on its reorganization as a unit of self-government. The old village republics are now only a memory and it was necessary to legislate for the new life. There are now village councils, block councils, based on the area of development blocks, and district councils. The pattern cannot be uniform and many state governments have been reluctant to shed their powers in favour of local self-government. Amendment of the Constitution is suggested to give constitutional sanction to local self-government councils, but that would mean too much legalism. It is better to build than to impose. In the village, caste has a more powerful hold than in the towns; conservatism and orthodoxy are unspent forces; the rich peasant is dominating; and the money-lender has an economic role. The credit system has to be introduced widely and uniformly and some change in social outlook has to come before the village community can feel it is a community. Party politics are a complicating factor. In Britain there was local self-government before there was national government. In India, elections at least at the district level and the block level mean political parties, and at the village level, there are the politics of caste, usury and the parish pomp. In China, with a one-party system, the party operates powerfully even at the village level, but in India the official machinery and the party agencies are in conflict and add to the tensions in the village.

There are 2·7 million members of village councils, 200,000 members of block councils and 5000 members of district councils. The official element is strongly mixed at the block and the district levels, and legislators are given a place. The political element is not disinterested enough and the official element not understanding enough, and the incentive of self-help is blunted. There is also confusion about names. Democratic decentralization sounds a fine phrase, but where planning is necessary even for new life in the villages and there can be no extension of electricity without regional planning, there has to be central direction before there can be decentralization. Many things, including dispensation of justice in petty disputes, can be left to the villagers, though Sir Henry Maine, nearly a hundred years ago, thought that only primitive justice was possible among them. There have to be enough resources for the Central Government, the state Government and the councils of local self-government, and at no level is taxation cheerfully undertaken. Discussion on forms becomes futile, when the problem is to create enough national wealth. The villages cannot live in isolation and miss the impact of the industrial revolution.

18. Bureaucracy and Bureaucratism

WITH or without Professor Parkinson's Law in operation, the situation in India may become similar to that in the later Roman Empire, when half of the population worked to feed the other half who administered it. The battalions of peons who stand like sentinels in the secretariat do not, of course, constitute bureaucracy. The core of the secretariat is the bureau of officials who exercise influence behind the noisy bastions of political power. Bureaucracy has ceased to be a system or an organization ; it is a state of mind, a mental hiatus. The etymological sense no longer matters, for through long practice, bureaucracy has developed special manners and habits. Its more outstanding products have many shining qualities, but they are also a part of a system. Carlyle, who had a prophet's sense about the most prosaic occupations, referred to " the continental nuisance called bureaucracy," and Lenin with leonine violence waged constant war on it. India has, with imitative indifference, borrowed from Britain the concept of the neutral civil servant who serves his successive political masters with equal fidelity and equal contempt. To the man in the street, bureaucracy means officialdom in all its crudely officious forms. But every country needs a bureaucracy so that the politicians can play, and every bureaucracy breeds bureaucratism, the essence of which is waste, delay and corruption. When bureaucracy operates on a gigantic scale, as in the big business of the Soviet Government and in the American Government of big business, bureaucratism is the law of life, occasionally disturbed by purges or senatorial investigation. This has no seasons or moods ; it is moodlessly endemic.

The involved, insidious manner of bureaucracy was well described by Themistocles. The Athenians, he said, governed the

Greeks; he governed the Athenians; his wife governed him; their son governed her. In the hierarchic progression between the minister and the under-secretary, it is difficult to know who governs; the clerk who prepares notes for the under-secretary need not be considered a mere notary, for he too is an important cog in a sleepily revolving wheel. When Napoleon asked his advisers to be speedy, to use despatch and not to forget that the world had been created in six days, he was protesting against the bureaucratic delays of his day. Bureaucracy also breeds verbosity and many verbal infelicities forbidden by the rules of rhetoric. Lord Curzon, the most efficient practitioner of authoritarianism under constitutional government, wrote pompously to the Secretary of State:

> Thousands of pages occupying hundreds of hours of valuable time are written every year by score upon score of officers, to the obfuscation of their own intellects and the detriment of their official work, and are then sent up to the local governments to be annotated, criticised and reported on by other officers who are similarly neglecting their duty in deference to this absurd tyranny; while finally this conglomeration of unassimilated matters comes up here to us again to be noted on in the departments of the Government of India.

The system, developed through a century of absent-mindedness, reminded Curzon of "a gigantic quagmire or bog, in which every question that comes along either sinks or is sucked down; and unless you stick a peg with a label over the part at which it disappeared, and from time to time go round and dig out the relics, you will never see anything of them again." There have been notes by Churchill, Vansittart and others on the need for pruning officialese into plain, understandable English, but bureaucracy has its own jargon and cannot do without it.

From distinguished servants of the East India Company like Charles Metcalfe and John Lawrence, the Indian Civil Service inherited its spacious, Victorian manner. The Lyalls and latter-day Butlers and Haileys were not only petty proconsuls, who pranced occasionally; they indulged in literary pursuits, writing even Pindaric odes, while playing golf and polo or sticking pigs. Their despatches were viceregal in their syntax. The bureaucracy of those days was paternalism in which minor military operations alternated with ballroom dancing as the main attractions. The empire rested on their ardent labours interrupted by rest in hill resorts. Their goal was retirement at the right age, with a seat, if possible, in the Secretary of State's Council.

In recent years, Indian bureaucracy has acquired stability, character, and, of course, obesity. It has its elaborate ritual of red tape ; in its fervent moods, it amounts to cabalistic mystery. It is a freemasonry of secret codes and sententious memoranda. The present-day bureaucrats are multi-purpose men ; the district administrators have not only to maintain law and order ; they must meet development targets. There is no proper demarcation of responsibility. The secretariat is more unwieldy and unworkable, too many stay too long, without contact with the people, and become draftsmen with elastic consciences. Some are forced to be courtiers. There were courtiers in Kipling's Simla, too, but they were encouraged to grunt dissent occasionally. The civil servant does not necessarily breed bureaucratism, but when ministers are not as competent or efficient as they should be, the permanent officials rock the cradles of government, and the cleverer of them know how to oblige ministers and oblige themselves. The best products from the universities still go into the services but they are no longer the best paid and better men are being attracted to the professions and business. The problem is to find enough of the best for every department of life. It was said of Newcastle, a sublime failure as a minister, that he was always doing business and never did it. In the progress towards socialism, the principle of civil service neutrality may mean public accountability for ministers and limited liability for officials. The bureaucracy, like its political masters, must adapt itself to the pressures of social change without giving up its right to give independent advice, but it is only a strong, efficient, political master that can make use of a strong, efficient bureaucrat.

19. Educating the Masters

THE Indian Constitution laid down that the state shall provide (by 1962) free and compulsory education for all children until they complete the age of fourteen years. The objective remains distant, for lack of funds, lack of schools, lack of teachers. The hunger for education is all-consuming and extends beyond the desire to be literate, and wherever there are schools, they are full. The smallest per cent increase in education means millions of new literates and this is a revolution in itself. In 1951–61 the number of students increased from 2·35 million to 4·35 million. During the Third Plan period, the total number of pupils at schools was expected to increase by 20·4 million. In 1951–61 the number of schools increased by 73 per cent from 230,555 to 398,200, and by the end of the Third Plan, the number of schools was to go up by 24 per cent to about 494,500. The largest increase is in primary schools, but high schools too were to go up by 5200. To maintain quality, along with this rate of physical expansion, is not easy. British reports on secondary education are not relevant to India where, apart from lack of funds and trained teachers, the medium of teaching and the pattern of languages, including Hindi and English, to be taught are problems. The standards of English in the secondary stage have fallen so low that they have affected the standards in universities and technical institutions.

The Robbins Report is relevant to the problem of numbers and quality in Indian universities. Restriction on admissions has been often suggested but has not proved practicable. In 1962–3 the total number of students in the universities and colleges rose to 1,272,666, an increase of 10·15 per cent over the enrolment for 1961–2; since 1954–5 the enrolment had doubled. The number of universities rose to 55 and the number of colleges,which absorbed nearly 85 per cent of the total enrolment, increased by 129. There is need for more universities, but it costs less to expand existing facilities than to set up new universities. Instead of the unitary pattern, a federal-unitary pattern is becoming fashionable, wherever resources and circumstances permit. The defects of instruction and the vagaries of the examination system add to the wastage. Lack of facilities for study and recreation increase an unrest born of intellectual and political discontent. The student politician has added disturbance to the uncreativeness of the teacher politician; both are products of wasteful conditions. The total number of teachers in the universities and colleges was 66,370, giving a teacher–pupil ratio of 1 to 16·3. There is shortage of competent and experienced teachers; they are underpaid and underequipped. The search for quality continues feebly; there are to be select centres of advanced study. The shortcomings are reflected in technological institutions, which are a poor preparation for the technological revolution.

Institutions grow with age, accumulating tradition, and Indian universities are not old enough. Taxila and Nalanda were among the oldest universities of the world, but they are now only ruins and memories. Oxford and Cambridge are ever venerable and ever new, like other old universities in Europe. American universities, even Yale and Harvard, are comparatively young, robust and affluent, and some of them, in spite of their large numbers, maintain high standards. Indian universities swung from liberal education to an education adapted to the needs of industrial life, and will take time to adjust themselves and wrest from contemporary turbulence academic temper. Some of the contrasts are striking. The Calcutta, Bombay and Madras universities, which have celebrated their centenaries, have achieved a serenity which the younger universities lack. There are no startling manifestations in them of the petty politics of teachers, of student indiscipline, or of steep falls from standards. If this were true only of the old universities of what were known as the presidency towns, it could be understood, but almost all south Indian universities are free from the infantilism which marks some of the north Indian universities. Among the new universities, Delhi is gathering standards, but it has the advantage of being a central university.

All universities now aspire to be central universities. The constitution-makers were right in making education a state subject, for the change in the medium of instruction from English to the regional language is important for the new generations, and the pace of displacement can be decided only in the state. State governments have, however, not been able to respect university autonomy to the extent that is possible, and they have extended not only party politics but personal ambitions into the campus. In the appointment of vice-chancellors, there have been few exceptions to political preference. Education ministers have not been enlightened people. Under the Constitution, the Centre has responsibility for the maintenance and co-ordination of standards and it can use its money power effectively, but it has no constitutional power to compel states to follow even agreed principles. Education was to be made a concurrent subject by amendment of the Constitution with the consent of the states, so that the Centre could legislate for education and the central laws could over-ride state laws. It is expected that concurrence can be achieved in a less startling way. Even Robbins could not have suggested a simple pattern for a country like India.

20. Science and Society

INDIA comes close to the scientific age once a while, during the annual sessions of the Science Congress. There is not a sufficiently strong social base for scientific activity and the scientific spirit or the scientific outlook will be an acquired appendage, till the mass of the people are close to science or its applied aspect, technology. The Government, the scientists, and the people are becoming aware of the relations between science and society, of the social purposes of science, and of the social responsibilities of scientists. Science has grown according to social needs and cannot escape the impact of the social environment. It cannot be merely theory; it has grown because of the need for action. Mercantilism led to the development of mathematics. The work of Galileo, Descartes and Newton laid the foundations of mechanics; thermodynamics had similar origins in social development, and most inventions followed military or naval requirements. It is good for science to be freed from slavery to military needs. Atom scientists have, however, to face the dilemma which conscience sometimes presents. The processes of atomic energy, for peaceful or destructive purposes, are the same up to a point. Life and death are thus inextricably mixed in the scientific process, and individual scientists cannot be left to make awful choices. They must submit themselves to social control and follow the discipline of social values. Doctrinal dogma is an aspect of social compulsions, but ideology has made no difference to the operation of scientific laws. There has been nothing like bourgeois physics or communist physics. It is in the organization and application of science that ideologies matter and social control has shown better results than the profit motive or the mere law of demand and supply.

Why did India, after many scientific achievements in the early years of the Christian era, make little progress thereafter? Some scientists attribute it largely to the importance given to the power of intuition and the authoritarian injunctions which made society rigid. The processes which were released by the Renaissance in Europe were not available for India; there was a paralysis of thought processes. But the reason why India lagged behind in scientific progress was, besides the super-abundance of non-scientific processes, the stratification of the economy and the lack of an urge for invention. With the importance given to liberal education by the British, there was little encouragement to science, and India became scientifically backward. British observers who pronounce India's agricultural doom must admit that India's problem is largely one of making up for the uncreative economic processes of British rule. India missed a century of economic progress, whatever she may have gained.

Any state which neglects scientific research now would be an archaic state, but science cannot be left entirely to the universities and to private industry. The advances in atomic and cosmic research and the cost and effort involved make state action inevitable. The lead which the Soviet Union has achieved in scientific education, research and development has made even American leaders of science admit the superiority of socialist organization with its subordination of private interest to public interest or state preferences in scientific priorities. But for the bias given in favour of rocketry, the Soviet Union would not have gone ahead of other countries in launching space satellites. This might be somewhat lopsided. But the American Society for Advancement of Science has had to admit that scientific research in the United States, under the direction of drug industries and others, too has been lopsided, that sciences like biology and bio-chemistry have been neglected, and that there should be some regulation of research. Mr. Harold Wilson and British Labour have given high priority to organized scientific revolution. The correct course for India in laying the technological foundations of society is to give a high priority to scientific education. The Government cannot be omniscient, even with a large array of scientific advisers, and would be capable of committing costly mistakes. Three myths have been too long encouraged. The first is that the scientist cannot look after the work of a scientific institute; the second is that managers and administrators of science are more valuable than scientists; the third is that it is easy for Indian scientists working abroad to find work in India. Science alone can point the way to the future but it has to be socially backed. Without a powerful state initiative, no country can attain an advanced place in scientific progress. Nothing else seems to matter so much.

21. *National Languages*

IN THE Eighth Schedule of the Indian Constitution, thirteen major Indian languages are enumerated, leaving aside the minor languages and hundreds of dialects described in scholarly detail by Grierson. The thirteen languages are mentioned only for two limited purposes. These languages are to be represented on the commission which the President of India is to appoint every five years to make recommendations on the progressive use of Hindi, in the place of English, for the official purposes of the Union and as the language of inter-state communication ; in the development of Hindi, the forms, style and expressions in the other languages are to be assimilated without interfering with its genius. Apart from Hindi, Sanskrit and Urdu, the other languages are important because they are the major regional languages with highly developed literatures, some much older than Hindi literature, and each is the language of a state of the Union. These unilingual states were inevitable, as the administration had to be in the language of the people in a democracy. Sanskrit is included as the language of ancient Indian civilization, from which all other Indian languages are derived.

There is still a debate whether Hindi and Urdu are separate languages or whether Urdu is only a form of Hindi ; this issue has been coloured by Hindu–Muslim cultural differences, though many Hindus treat Urdu as their language. Hindustani is the basic speech from which, according to some, Hindi and Urdu developed ; to others, Urdu was the camp language of Muslim rulers, the basis of which was Hindi. Gandhi advocated the cause of Hindustani, with Hindi and Urdu as its two forms with two different scripts ; so did Jawaharlal Nehru. At the time of constitution-making,

Hindi was adopted as the language of the Union, and an attempt was made to define its content, as a language representing the composite culture of India, assimilating the forms, style and expressions used in Hindustani and other languages. The Constitution was concerned with the use of Hindi only for the official purposes of the Union and as the language of communication between the states. But official purposes include the language to be used in the administration, in the law courts and in the schools and universities, and official purposes could enforce style and forms, whatever may be the usages of literature.

The displacement of English is not by Hindi alone, for at the regional level, the state languages take the place of English. There is thus a tussle not only between Hindi and English but between Hindi and the other Indian languages. The problem is complicated because Hindi is the language of many states, which are contiguous, and each of the other languages has only one state in which it could be the medium. Hindi fanaticism, which gathered force after independence, created the impression that Hindi was to be imposed, and there has been resistance and even a threat of secession. But Hindi has not yet been used for all official purposes even in the Hindi states, and it is admitted that like other Indian languages, it has to be further developed not only for official but scientific and technological purposes. The deadline laid down in the Constitution for the use of Hindi has had to be postponed by a law permitting the continued use of English.

Some Indian language had to take the place of English some time at the Union level, and by what was known as a constitutional settlement, arrived at after much debate at the time of constitution-making, Hindi was adopted, though it secured only a majority of one vote against Hindustani in the Congress. There is a consensus that there can be no hurry about displacement of English by Hindi, that the non-Hindi areas must be also ready for it, and that, apart from sentiment, there are questions of practical convenience, like the medium of examination for recruitment to the all-India services. The non-Hindi languages, because of their importance, are all called national languages, and these languages will take the place of English in the states, possibly as the medium even in the university stage. The unsettled questions are when Hindi will take the place of the regional languages, at what stage in the universities, at what stage in the courts, at what stage in the administration? There is no clear answer. There has to be a time-table of displacement but there is none yet. The importance of English has been increasingly recognized, as the most convenient international medium, as a part of the Indian heritage, and as the language of modern knowledge. Everyone wants it as a second or third language to be taught as early as possible and learnt well for international use, but no one is certain when it can be given up for science or in the courts. English will be learnt and spoken by larger numbers of people, as literacy spreads, and there is a demand for cutting out the present literacy lumber and teaching it as a second language, when it is being accepted as the second language in most non-English countries.

There are few lucid intervals in the unceasing war waged on English by some Indians, but the drive for displacing English finds it getting entrenched like the Duke of Wellington at Torres Vedras. Language, even where it is not the mother tongue, can be an intimate part of life, and its literature a part of the make-up of the mind. But the Indian *petit bourgeoisie* find it necessary to do penance for their original sins; so English classes must be boycotted, English sign-boards must be removed, English letters should be defaced or blacked out. Even in China, the communists have allowed sign-boards in English to remain over shops in Shanghai and Nanking and the Chinese language flourishes unenfeebled by fanaticism. English in India, is, of course, different; it has become embedded in Indian life and it is easier for Indians to say in English what sounds like Greek in the Indian languages. The explosive eloquence of Indian delegates at the United Nations was buttressed with quotations from neglected English classics like Burke.

Too many Indians are Indo-Anglians. Thomas Babington Macaulay, with his rhetorical minute on education, decreed this destiny for them, and since then some Indians, behaving as if to their eternal regret their mother tongue was not English, want it also to be declared a national language. Every educated Indian becomes another Indo-Anglian when he is educated with the help of Nesfield grammar and Macmillan readers. It has meant mesmerized articulation, though at the end of it all, an Indian might feel only slightly more omniscient than Sam Weller who, after learning the alphabet, wondered whether it was worth going through so much to know so little. Indo-Germanic philology shows how English, by a process of moulting, evolved from barbaric splendour into a free, simple speech as modern as anything that can be invented today. Indians have learnt it with passion for two centuries and they should not unlearn it, but some unlearning is involved in the deteriorating standards of teaching and textbooks and in the disappearance of the English-speaking community. It required a national effort to produce an English-educated élite to run the country or to produce scientists who could become Fellows of the Royal Society. Such wholesale absorption was a tragedy of extravagance and waste. There are Indo-Anglians who think they can manufacture their own brand of English like Americans and other English-speaking peoples. Indian English can only be bad English.

The anti-English mood of fanaticism is gone for good, except among a few who think that if English goes Hindi will flourish and become the *lingua franca ;* a more sober mood of living with English and its eccentricities permanently has developed. It is recognized as a language which Indians should value for technological progress at least, and it will have to remain an associate language of Hindi as long as the people of the non-Hindi regions want it. The spirit of Kipling which still stirs uneasily in his Benmore home in Simla might rejoice over this consummation of British influence. The Indian people are expected to be fond of learning languages, and bilingual and trilingual feats are recommended to them. There is yet no disenchantment with English, and for a long time, the Indian languages, in spite of the prize money that is being pumped into them, might not offer half the enchantments of English.

22. A Press for the People

THE Indian press has many shortcomings, but the shortcomings which the public think they know are not the important ones. The press is utterly inadequate for the country's needs. The Registrar of Newspapers, in his latest report, published in August 1964, says that there were 7790 newspapers and periodicals on record; the ascertainable circulation for 4750 of them was 202·91 lakhs. Five hundred and three of them were daily newspapers, twenty-two more than the previous year's figure of 481, with an ascertainable circulation for 345 daily newspapers of 55·79 lakhs. Daily newspapers in English continued to command the highest circulation, 14·52 lakhs or 26 per cent of the total circulation of all daily newspapers. Daily newspapers in Hindi, numerically the largest group, came second with a total circulation of 7·64 lakhs; then follow daily newspapers in Malayalam, Marathi, Gujarati and other Indian languages. There was only one newspaper in Assamese with a circulation of 7000. The circulation, in spite of auditing and rechecking, are not strictly verifiable, but they cannot be larger than what the newspapers themselves claim. Five, six or seven million copies of daily newspapers for a population of 450 million is a depressingly low figure. Japan is most advanced in Asia and countries like Egypt have far larger circulations. Large areas of Hindi-speaking India are backward in literacy and whatever literacy there is has not been fully converted into readership. The absence of metropolitan towns in Uttar Pradesh, Bihar, Madhya Pradesh and Rajasthan has not helped, while Hindi newspapers from Delhi and Calcutta have been able to command good circulations. In states like Kerala, without metropolitan towns, both literacy and readership are high. It is not merely a matter of readership or newspaper techniques. In 1962 there had been a momentum of growth in circulations because of the Chinese invasion and the general elections; in 1963 the rate of increase came down. For some years, the difficult foreign exchange position and the need to ration newsprint have inhibited growth.

There has been a tendency to concentration of ownership, though it is difficult to say how much there is of it. The Registrar of Newspapers says that six newspapers owned by big business enjoyed a monopolistic position. Big business has been operating in the newspaper industry powerfully since the war. The Indian Rockefellers, Fords and Nuffields have been in it, by the side of the Indian Beaverbrooks, and this has inhibited competition. The Registrar of Newspapers says that nine newspaper owners, with four chains, three groups, and two multiple units, among them, published forty-three daily newspapers and commanded a total circulation of 23·35 lakhs or 41 per cent of the total circulation of daily newspapers. Nobody knows what is to be done about it, for the attachment to freedom is so strong that government interference is not wanted. Yet the increasing concentration of newspaper ownership is seen as a threat to the democratic process. Change in newspaper ownership can come about only as part of a change in the economic structure, but newspaper combines are powerful enough to oppose any significant change. Diffusion of ownership is accepted in theory, but the high cost of machinery and newsprint, the rising wage bill, and competition from metropolitan centres inhibit the growth of newspaper in regional and district centres. Political ownership has not affected the pattern. The Congress with twenty-nine newspapers commands only a circulation of 27,483, the Communist Party with twenty-five newspapers commands a circulation of 82,920 and the Socialist Party has a few newspapers with little circulation.

The Indian press has had two traditions, the tradition of nationalism and the tradition of Fleet Street. The results have been incongruous. After independence, nationalism is not the force it was and Fleet Street seems remote. There are newspapers which maintain standards, though the tendency is towards a timid sobriety.

Technical skills and social awareness have been growing in the profession, but with limited circulations and an appeal restricted to the intelligentsia, there is no popular appeal and no sense of social responsibility. News follows the cult of personality and the sensation of social and economic change is not yet considered a worthwhile sensationalism. As circulations grow and newspapers have to cater to mass readership, both techniques and values may change, increasing the appeal of vulgarity and spurious sensationalism. There is no self-regulation in the industry and the profession has not established articulate processes of self-criticism. The operation of freedom of expression within the framework of an industry will present more awkward problems in India than elsewhere.

The newspapers have also not succeeded in smoothing the information processes, in spite of an occasional bizarre display of prosperity. New jargon, partly borrowed from the discarded traditions of the west, has damaged clarity and made information unreliable. There is too much reliance on reference to mysterious sources like "informed circles", "knowledgeable circles", "official circles", "unofficial circles", "certain circles" and "some circles", geometry which is not a good guide and is not made more reliable with the additions of terms like "official quarters". The English language is a difficult medium for Indians, but the struggle against hackneyed phrases like "the irony of fate", "the psychological moment" or "the logic of facts" should be as grim as in Britain or the United States. The Indian languages have their own semantic problems. It has yet to be understood that the press deals not only with men and events but with words, and that all aspects of communication are important. Information has not yet been given enough importance in India and government information sources with their spoon-feeding are smothering the smaller newspapers. The reaction is to treat facts as free and comment as sacred.

Political articulation is easy in India because of the too many statements, often repetitive and personal, made by politicians and because of question-hour in the legislatures. In the United States, where there are no interpellations in the legislatures, there is a greater burden on the reporter or columnist, and the White House and the president's press conferences have led to a tradition of skilful and reliable reporting. The presidents can help. Wilson was a phrase-maker, Harding coined the atrocious word " normalcy ", Franklin Roosevelt had his " forgotten man " and " social security ". But the sources were often " White House spokesman ", and in Harding's case the " spokesman " was himself. When Roosevelt introduced the practice of quoting what the president said at press conferences, " a White House source " or " a source close to the administration " was no longer needed, and in Eisenhower's time, James Hagerty was an undaunted and identified source. Jawaharlal Nehru's press conferences, informal, impromptu affairs, helped circulation of information. Most newspapers, however, now have more than the purpose of communication to serve, and many are finding it useful to mix opinion columns and news columns and to mix opinion and news in all columns. Freedom of information has, however, not been a free affair and has been an item of the cold war in UNESCO and at the United Nations.

23. *Reluctant Dragon*

THE plight of the middle classes in India, which has produced much pathos, is related to the plight of Indian democracy. High taxation and high cost of living are causing misery to the middle classes, while the rich are looking after themselves well and the lower classes have secured a rise in their earnings. What is " middle " about the middle classes ? Aristotle stated their position in his *Politics*:

> Thus it is manifest that the best political community is formed by citizens of the middle class, and that those states are likely to be well-administered, in which the middle class is large, and larger if possible than both the other classes, or at any rate than either singly, for the addition of the middle class turns the scales, and prevents either of the extremes from being dominant. Great then is the good fortune of a state in which the citizens have made a moderate and sufficient property, for where some possess much, and the others nothing, there may arise an extreme democracy, or a pure oligarchy; or a tyranny may grow out of either extreme democracy, or out of an oligarchy . . . and where the middle class is large, there are least likely to be fractions and dissensions.

Aristotle's logic sounds modern but his experience was limited. In modern times the middle classes first emerged in Britain and other European countries. They had their historical origin in trade, in the free professions, and in the Industrial Revolution. They were responsible for extension of the franchise. Cobden and Bright and Morley and the Chamberlains of Birmingham were the products of the mercantile and machine age. The people, who with their guilt complex were responsible for Lloyd George's budget, who fought the Boer War, who manned the Fabian Society and who led the Labour Party, were their successors. They are now more extensively spread, more diversified and splintered in their economy, and seek their spiritual liberation in more multifarious ways than they did in the days of Ruskin, Carlyle and Morris.

The Indian middle classes did not come into their own through two centuries of foreign rule. They were largely foreign-created middle classes, most of them salaried, with no substantial economic base, and with no tradition. The Gandhis and Tagores were exceptions to the rule of uncreativeness. But the middle classes are plural in India, as in other countries, and there are the upper middle and the lower middle classes, the lower middle becoming the upper middle as a napkin becomes a serviette. There is no single middle class, upper or lower, and there are social distinctions even between members of the same class. The family and not the individual is the clue to class, and a class does not emerge from a mere economic condition but has a class style, a way of living and thinking. In the case of the middle classes, it is summed up in the term *bourgeoisie* who, whatever might be the applicability of Nancy Mitford's "U" and "non-U" to Indian conditions, can be formidable as leaders of respectability, smugness and stability, and whose condition is the concern of those who want to dam revolution and prevent the rise of communism. The *bourgeoisie* have their virtues, including Philistinism, but it is only now that the Indian *bourgeoisie* are emerging, with the initiation of the Industrial Revolution. Even then the *bourgeoisie* are fragile, for a salariat and standards of life can be swept away. It is a way of life represented largely by teachers, lawyers, doctors, engineers, officials and clerks; it is when the way of life is adopted also by artisans, business men and managers, shopkeepers and traders, and farmers, partaking of the flux of social mobility, that the middle classes acquire the character of the *bourgeoisie.* The process permits of much upstartism. Even permit-holders, who become rich overnight through the patronage of politicians, add to the process. The much-discussed corruption of the day is largely a part of the struggle to achieve class, even transcending caste.

The stratification of the middle classes into the *bourgeoisie* has become the concern of sociologists and grumblers who have no taste for revolution. An Indian finance minister peevishly said that the middle classes are not being abolished merely because of the application of the taxation theories of Kaldor. The middle classes are hit by high prices and do not find their salaries rising equally high, but they are partners in the regime. The present attempt is equalization among the upper middle classes in the race for development and also as an insurance against revolution. It has been said that between England and revolution there will always stand an army of bowler hats. But pauperization of lower middle classes may lead to a revolution by them. It is a development which even communists cannot thoughtlessly encourage, for it may take a fascist direction. There has been so far one middle-class revolution in India. The 1942 revolution, which was a middle-class revolution betrayed by the middle classes, was not genuine because the middle classes were not genuine. The next middle-class revolution, whatever working-class blood it may contain, may end in dictatorship, not of the proletariat. The middle classes are a reluctant dragon which will strike at what it is too weak to resist and then find that it faces death.

24. The Secular Idea

THEOCRATIC states are not possible in the modern world, apart from what the Pope makes of Vatican City. But the secular idea had to be propagated in India, when separate electorates based on communities existed, when the country was divided on the basis of religion, and when Pakistan was being proclaimed an Islamic state. The Cambridge *History of India* says: " The name for India in the Avesta is Hindu, which, like the old Persian Hi(n)du, is derived from the river Indus, Sanskrit Sindu—the designation of the stream being transferred to the territory adjacent to it and its tributaries." The name " Hindu ", for the people and for the religion, was given by the Muslim invaders and conquerors. It could be applied to all Indians before Islam and other religions came, but it can no longer be so applied. The increasing integration of the diverse elements of the country has to be based on secularism, and socialism, which Parliament adopted, is a secular idea. Unity in diversity is the essence of national integration, but Hindu revivalists want a unity based on a monolithic structure. To them all Indians are Hindus; the Indian nation is the Hindu nation. This is anachronistic, even as mere linguistics.

Secularism means that no one following any particular religion would suffer any disability in the eye of law and that men of all religions will have equal opportunities, privileges, and rights under the Constitution. This is what secularism should mean to all secularists, but some Hindus draw a distinction between their secularism and non-communal secularism by attributing all possible virtues to one religion above all religions. Gandhi was the most religious-minded of men and his attempt was to spiritualize politics, but he affirmed the universality of all religions and did not think that all religions were equal only in the eye of law. Muslim conventions and Hindu conventions and what has been happening in several places in India should remind people of the dangers of religious denomination, apart from the need for religion or the value of any religion. Not enough has been done to secularize life in India. Even if the priestly castes do not intrude into politics directly, their hold on the minds of people is great and not apolitical. The Christian church has had a long record in secular progress everywhere, but politics are not free from the influence of the organized church. There has been greater timidity in India after freedom towards separation of religion from politics.

Indian secularism is not yet secular enough. It is not even strident anti-clericalism. Hinduism, which was known for many protestant movements, is losing its philosophical inspiration and becoming ritual more than ever and Islam in India seems to have lost its capacity for introspection. If these major religions become petrified, they become an inert institutional background and cease to have any relation to social and economic change. That may provide stability and keep religion in the background, but they choke social and economic change, and even when the Pope is adumbrating democratic socialism by encyclicals, Hindu and Muslim politics have become doublefaced, looking forward to change and looking forward to religion, which means caste, conservatism and priesthood. Even Marxist socialist parties, which should be bold sociologically, are afraid of attacking the social fabric, which is buttressed with religion, because they are afraid not only of the law which prohibits promotion of enmity between religious communities but of the hold of religion on life. Religion predominates in all contemporary philosophy, especially Indian philosophy. The religion of man has not replaced the religion of gods.

There has been progress towards secularism, but it has not been spectacular. Hindu law has been stripped of its scriptural formalism which made it a deadweight on the evolution of Hindu society, but secularism would mean a common civil code, and though Hindu personal law has been codified, personal laws remain.

While freedom of faith and the right to manifest faith are the subjects of inquiry by United Nations' agencies so that there should be no discrimination and persecution, India has not put religion in the place where it should belong. The failure of political parties to absorb adequately people of all religions into their fold is a shortcoming of Indian secularism. Muslim conventions are an aberration and not a danger without separate electorates, and Hindu conventions, in seeking to perform the impossible task of reducing a vast federation of faiths into a political caucus, make no sense. Indians may be still distant from the secular idea as a non-religious attitude to life's problems. Britain has an established church, but the British people are secular in a sense in which the Indian people are not yet. The secularist provisions of non-discrimination in the Constitution are not enough; it provides recognition of institutions with religious denomination. The secular outlook is nothing less than the scientific outlook.

25. *A Mandarin Class*

SOMERSET MAUGHAM may have derived benefit from Radhakrishnan's books on Indian philosophy, but the Indian intellectual is largely an Indo-English intellectual, a product of the British impact. In recent times the Indian intellect has expressed itself mainly through English and there is a good amount of semantic confusion in the Indian renaissance. But the Sanskrit or Persian scholar has not protected his intellectual integrity merely by denying himself the knowledge that is available in English. The intellect can work through any language. The intellectual process, however, is not always a creative process. If it is genuine, it can generate movements of thought which will affect not only thinking but action. Fluency of expression in English has given a false impression of the Indian capacity to think originally or creatively. The imitativeness of Indian scholarship is apparent in the dowdy books produced, though there are scholars who are not imitative. Not all the scholarship has bred a genuine scholasticism in the country because the intellectual process is not always genuine. Little mandaris sit in seats of authority and lay down the law for the intellect. The three autonomous academies, for letters, for music, and for fine arts, which are financed by the Government and are subject to auditing by officials of the Finance Ministry do not make an athenaeum, and academicians who have not staged even a single battle of the intellect cannot be expected to provide intellectual stimulus. Professors and deans and vice-chancellors have been somewhat mean manifestations of the intellect.

The phase of pseudo-intellectualism which has its roots in the universities is being prolonged because there is too much of sounding brass in the set-up. In no other country is the pure intellect so disregarded, and since the applied intellect is measured by success of the kind which the Philistines, who are generally the rulers, can easily recognize, opportunism has acquired value. The man who opens his mouth most at the conference table is the wisest and is often the chairman; he reduces intellectual activity to rules and by-laws with bureaucratic efficiency. Charles Snow has pointed out how two cultures have developed, the culture of science and the culture of the humanities, each not knowing the language of the other; there is also the language of the bureaucracy which understands no other language. The genuine intellectuals are outnumbered by the increasing crowd of votaries of the intellect, who at best are content to express themselves in intelligible English and think that they can think because they can cerebrate weakly, quote profusely or translate into their own idiom some of the western thinkers.

The Indian political parties cannot be expected to be anything more than copies, intellectually. The Congress is the only organization which seems indigenous with a core of originality because Gandhi endowed it with abundant Indianness. Socialist parties, Marxist–Leninist or not, derived their inspiration from the west and are not yet able to become wholly Indian in modes of thinking. Indian socialism derives far more from the west even now than from Indian sources or the Indian context. Ricardo and Marx cannot be eliminated from modern economics, but political and social organization can be more Indian than alien. When any idea takes shape, it is related to western thinkers and thought, because their language is more familiar and political philosophy in particular cannot do much without the help of language. To be intellectual is to doubt, to test, to dissent and despair and not to come to easy and convenient conclusions. Dogmatism has become natural to Indian intellectuals who cannot bear the strain of the intellectual process and find it easy and pleasurable to be pseudo-intellectuals. Indian political statements are assertions devoid of thought and unargued aphorisms, and that is at least one reason why political activity is not action and takes often the form of marches and hunger-strikes. The leaders are afraid that thinking might lead to too much doubt and that scepticism at the top might lead to inaction among the mass. This is denial of existence. If the intellectual must be a passionate sceptic, the more the passionate scepticism is embedded in political parties, the more they should be able to be true to themselves and to the ideas which they seek to serve. It is easy for the irresponsible to be brilliant; it is easier to be brilliant by being irrelevant. This is not the proper intellectual base for political action. The intellect can find exercise in the wide open spaces and not in the cribbed atmosphere of the coffee houses.

The Indian tradition is to honour both mental and supramental processes. The first stages of industrial advance should have led to a widespread spirit of inquiry, not protestations of weak and indisciplined wills but a rousing Lutheran challenge. Free inquiry should be in the social and religious sphere, but a dull dread has become established because people think more of convenience than of the conscience. The result is that irreligion and superstition smother the little there is of the scientific spirit, which should be logic *in excelsis*. The age of reason or the age of enlightenment has its horrors, for the intellect can be a treacherous instrument and it is difficult to judge whether Voltaire's wisecracks or mistresses are more interesting. But reasoning is of value, if man is not merely to progress from one dark age to another for lack of logic. The intellect needs bouts of insanity if it has to be tempered, and when integrity is developed from temper, it may be possible to survive the magical terrors of technology.

There are social discrepancies which undermine the pride of intellect. Even the third-rate politician makes greater noise and attracts greater attention than leading scientists or philosophers. The M.P.s with their privileges of all kinds, about seven hundred of them, with their allowances, concessions and amenities, the miscellaneous crowds of ministers, the senior officials who overflow the airways and the railroads, will for a long time take precedence over the intellectual. Politics, according to eminent British practitioners, is " one long second-best ", but it continues to be the first-best in India and ministers inaugurate scientific and literary conferences in insulting pomp. To take the issue to a higher level, for a long time, the question has been asked: if you had your choice, would you rather have been Gibbon or Pitt, Macaulay or Palmerston—or, in Indian terms, Tagore or Gandhi? The question can be variously answered according to one's idea of the nature of fame. The Indian politician is a semi-intellectual, a man in a hurry with no time to think, but he is the patron of poets, the writer of prefaces, and the arbiter of academic life. It will be tragic if Titus Oates, legislator or minister, tries every time to take precedence over everyone else.

26. Intellectuals at Bay

THE Indian Renaissance was a latter-day affair, and while it witnessed the efflorescence of the intellect, it has been limited by conformity first to nationalism and now to political doctrine. The Indian intellectual, who lustily sang " God Save the King ", was willing to join the ranks of political sansculottism and is now willing to be conscripted in the name of culture. Aristotle thought man was a rational animal because some people could do sums, but man did many more things. With the scientific discoveries of Copernicus and the geographical discoveries of Columbus and others, new worlds opened, cosmology and other subjects were recovered from revelation, and the intellect struggled for liberty from dogma and superstition. It took nearly two centuries for science and philosophy to acquire the rationalist temper, and then the revolution in social and economic organization led to the bitter and prolonged war for intellectual liberty. The war is not ended, for new gods and new revealed religions have arisen.

The intellectual in India as elsewhere is now essentially a middle-class product. He is subject to the grinding machinery of mass production and is not independent of the laws of wages and prices. The industrial process, the planning process, the democratic process are not helping the intellectual process. Not all intellectuals are alienated from the people and not all of them are on sale, but there is no character among them probably because they are products too much of general education and too little of the spirit of science.

The Indian artist is perplexed and driven to cults and coteries. The state must see that artists do not starve or die indigently, but a socialist society should mean that no one, not merely artists, should die indigently. It is one thing to look after the artist physically, another to look after him intellectually. In socialist societies the Pasternaks have no life outside society, except that they can live wrapt in their own vision, but the artists may claim the right to be unsocial in a society which is changing too slowly. The state may create an atmosphere of free communication, though it can become stifling, and arrange for recognition, but the machinery of recognition can never be adequate and all possible recognition need not mean that all the good artists are recognized in good time. The trouble with the awards given by the academies is not that they are inadequate but that they are artificial as evidence of recognition of values. The artist is no longer wholly the free spirit of the regenerate days of the Indian Renaissance, which produced a Tagore and many hairy imitations of him. The artist is now somewhat of a social figure, and a socialite, who has been recognized and reprocessed in foreign countries for his devotion to cultural freedom or to peace. The economic well-being of a few artists is, however, different from the invocation of the creative possibilities of the people as a whole to produce artists from the widest possible social base. The élite is becoming wider now ; it need not mean that it is necessarily more creative than the older, and smaller, élite. The growing means of mass communication offer the artist ampler opportunities ; still he is not reaching a proportionately larger number of people. There are larger number of devotees of art cults but there is little art criticism. The academies and awards are a part of the speeding up of the processes of art communication, not necessarily of the processes of aesthetic communication.

Indian writing is divided in spirit. In a world divided in commitment, there is fear of commitment, and there is fear of freedom too, though the writer must be free to be creative. The detonation of war on the border did not help creation. It is only after a war that its literature is produced. Homer came long after the Trojan war, and the *Mahabharata*, India's great war epic, came long after the Mahabharata war. Yet the writer cannot be insensitive even to the undertones of war. The American Civil War is said to have been the first modern war and Walt Whitman, who responded warmly to it, the first modern poet. The writer in war-time is, however, essentially a propagandist, boosting somebody's morale, tightening his guts, or mourning his gutlessness. Indian writing, flapped drily within newspapers, reverberating hollowly through the radio or issuing with adjectival vigour in press notes and pamphlets, was propaganda ; with little that was creative in it, it was not even good propaganda. Without the flesh of facts, it was feeble, and without the blood of passion, it was pallid. Neither was it positive, for all writers were busy reacting to Peking instead of making Peking react to them. It is not necessary that the aggressor should be more creative ; shattered, disillusioned spirits should have something more to say. Only a soldier-poet from the Sela Pass could have given expression to the terror and sweetness of loneliness and death among high snows, not people who were busy making something of their remoteness from bullets. It was fear of commitment, of freedom, even of opportunity. The writer who withdrew into himself or the writer who wrote merely from ancient commitment would write little of value ; the result was as barren as barrack-room ballads. The free writer is in a better position than the committed writer and the committed writer is freer than the mercenary writer, but no song of the day has yet stirred the Indian nation.

The greatest novel about war dealt with peace also. Tolstoy was a Titan and his appetites were gargantuan. There is nothing Tolstoyan about any of the Indian literatures, and after freedom, literary values have become artificial. There is little of movement, even of political movement. Probably there is no need to expect literature of value in tense times. But China may not leave the Indians to a sterile silence ; she may move the sleeping genius of a peace-loving people to some loud utterance that will linger when the present generation is gone. Literature is, partly, lingering remembrance of things past.

27. *Tradition and Taste*

THERE is something to be said for sensations, and Indian life now has few sensations which are not political. A life of that kind cannot be a full life. There is feebleness of feeling and expression in a country which in its centuries-long placidity had its protests and challenges. Religion, among a people who have been proud of their popes, is divorced from philosophy and is more of a ritual than ever, and philosophers are mere professors. Literature, in spite of the prizes that are given, has no movement, apart from the self-torment of individuals with abundant egoism but no afflatus. The artist is a Van Gogh or a Picasso in pose, normal in his cultivated abnormality, imitatively original or an imitation of an imitation. Social unrest is sought to be mopped up by grants from social welfare boards. In science, shoddy solar cookers are giving place slowly to supersonic planes. For the world, this cannot, of course, be the age of Leonardo da Vinci or of the steam engine. In Indian terms, this cannot be the age of Nalanda, where a great university flourished centuries ago, or even the age of Rabindranath Tagore, but it should be an age capable of sensations, and the sensations are getting stifled by politics.

The milder sensations are often transferred to Parliament because they can be best expressed in words and do not find expression in the popular mood. The controversy over the history of the freedom movement will make no difference to Indian history or any other history, though if there had been lustiness in the Indian historical method, it would have been an event in histriography. No history of any freedom movement, unless it is part of the history of a successful ideology, can be imposed on the people ; it has to satisfy different standards. Nor can anyone hope to be a syndicate and produce detailed and learned but prolix chronicles like the Cambridge histories. It would be a one-man history if it were the work of one man, a dull compendium if he were a mere literary agent, and controversial, even one-sided, if he were to enjoy freedom. Even the abridged Gibbon has his critics, apart from the original Gibbon, for wrong abridgment. It was good there was a public controversy on history, which in recent years has not been one of India's achievements and has remained largely unreadable.

India is not yet very modern but is over-ridden with what is known as modern art. The Academy of Fine Arts was blamed in Parliament for encouraging what is supposed to be alien, abstract, subjective, impressionist or expressionist. The name does not matter, not even the cult, in an age of cults. Modern art, as it has come to be known long after it ceased to be modern in other countries, is recognizable in the angular, piecemeal, Picasso-like shapes in painting and the bric-à-brac of bronze and plaster which signifies nothing more than what it is supposed to signify. Form emerges from formlessness, there can be expressiveness in all kinds of expression, and there is always a desire to escape from what is stereotyped. The counter-protest is probably against filling the land with ugly and meaningless forms. At an international art exhibition held in New Delhi, a canvas with over a hundred pen-knife incisions was considered an outstanding example of modern art. The number of incisions were counted because it was thought that school-children going to the exhibition might be attracted to add one or two more. It is difficult to say whether modern art is the fashion of the moment, an inevitable projection of modern life or a reflection of personality trying to be true to itself. The academy may not be able to control modernism of many kinds, if it is real, and it is good that there is some thinking about it, some sensation. There was modern art in all ages and it slowly became classical. Modern art is not accepted wholly even in the industrially advanced countries for there something modern is found in the old. Art criticism in India is not sharp and nobody seems to know what is modern in modern art.

Musical taste also is under discussion. All India Radio has become a means of popularizing classical music which was popular before it became classical and an exclusive preserve of the élite, but film songs, which, too, AIR makes popular, have become distasteful for their erotic appeal and occasional vulgarity. AIR has been asked to be not only a mass medium but an arbiter of taste. Neither academies nor state-run organizations like AIR can undertake formulation or standardization of taste unless society is to be less free than it is. Even where the state or a subsidiary body can give a direction to art, it would be difficult to give a direction to taste, though the erring artists can suffer from contracted or closed means of communication. The state is depriving the élite of their influence without ensuring wider participation by the people. Art and art criticism are in danger of becoming strait-laced and losing their spontaneity. If art is to depend on contracts and mechanically done scripts, there may be utter lack of standards and what AIR and academies set may be the only possible standards. The qualities of Indian art will continue to be elusive till there is enough of sturdy, living art capable of excess, instead of suffering from neurosis and feebleness of forms.

28. *Culture and Anarchy*

THERE is an Indian culture, though it has many strands. Culture transcends all art forms, while containing all of them. There is nothing like Indian literature; there are Indian literatures. No person can hope to write a history of Indian literature, as one could write a history of English literature or French literature, because there are many Indian languages with rich literatures. In other ways Indian culture presents common features, with only two main traditions of music, with half a dozen schools of dance, with not many schools of architecture, sculpture or painting. It can no longer be said that the middle class has not the will or the power to be creative; it is a maturing class. The effect of economic processes on culture cannot yet be exactly measured, and anthropology, which shyly draws upon primitive and semi-primitive life, does not help in tracing cultural forms. The primitive is considered genuine and the search for genuineness continues, but it has led to florid imitations of folk dance and folk music. The folk are happy with their dancing and singing in their local habitations, but the town dwellers must remove their guilt complex and absolve themselves of their sense of sin and alienation by urban versions of what they think is folk culture. This culminates in the grand mixture of the genuine and the spurious in Republic Day folk dances in New Delhi, with state capitals arranging for regional mixtures.

The New Delhi élite reserve their ecstasies for genuine visitations, the Vienna Philharmonic, Berlin ensembles, Vietnamese dancers or Oxford players rendering Shakespeare. The native culture is promoted by organizations like All India Radio, the national academies, and a strange assortment of theatre groups. Everything is done almost in winter, a season which is not cold in most parts of the country and gives the folk of the capital the feeling of warmth and woollen insensibility. There is much trafficking in culture. Art is advertised more than practised, and many artists exhibit themselves and are not inspired by the spirit that leads to Broadway in New York or the National Theatre in London. Patrons look very patronizing. The genuine artists cannot afford to live in New Delhi, enveloped by the orient-minded curiosity of too many embassies. The result largely is a culture of sorts.

New Delhi, with its personality cult, is capable of producing culture almost like cabbage. It is mostly manifestation. Ministers are the new ogres of culture and a cultural show where the president and the prime minister are present is a success. In their desire to do everything possible, these and other patrons do not often know what they do. Every country has its metropolitan culture, but New Delhi is still a colony, a small town, with a small town mentality and with small-minded hierarchies. In such a place, culture is like soilless cultivation. State patronage or any patronage is inimical to authenticity, unless state and people are one and culture has not become a closed shop. Ram Lila, which presents in a popular form the *Ramayana*, the ancient epic which tells the story of Rama, perhaps is the only meeting ground between the classes ; it is dated but it lives. What else is possible ? It should be possible to preserve the small virtues and some integrity. Newspapers indiscriminately deal in art criticism and have created a new class of art critics who clothe their inanities in English. The reviews are padded with the appropriate jargon, but there is no respect for standards. Blurb writers are in league with promoters and managers of culture.

It is sham amateurism. Indian culture needs the core of professionalism, except in music in which the professionals excel. AIR has made professionalism of amateurs but it has also made amateurs of professionals. There is more twilight than light in a transition and the leading dancers and musicians who lent charm to feudalism are almost all gone. British viceroys and governors enjoyed waltz or foxtrot in banqueting halls and the ruling princes arranged feasts of music by virile baritones. Nautch was performed by genuine nautch girls. Classical Indian dance has been rediscovered and re-presented, but the best that New Delhi can see comes from little-known places in the states where tradition has been preserved assiduously and with slender means. There are several schools of austerity, especially in the south, where artistic values are maintained with a sense of integrity, but this is not possible in New Delhi, where art is a series of shows to which school children are compelled to contribute their toddling footwork. Genius may be spreading like a disease under the propulsion of patrons, but the show business is still a manifestation, beside which Elvis Presley would seem precise.

29. *New Babylon?*

NEW DELHI, built on the ruins of seven old Delhis, is fast becoming a New Babylon. Anything is a sensation in that camp-like atmosphere of a society adhering to a secretariat; a meaningless suicide, a lovers' quarrel, a minor strike, a fashion parade or a bus collision. Pomp and extravagance were once royal; they were then gubernatorial; now they are mostly ministerial and the private lives of ministers are becoming public. That is probably some gain. Ministers have a gruelling time and are ridiculed or abused; they have to answer questions in Parliament and must blabber even when they need not; they have to inaugurate something or other and keep their constituents pleased. Few ministers spend sleepless nights and fewer suffer in health. Still, if they are asked to be sparing in their use of electricity and water, they feel like going on strike.

There is something in the Good Life. It should be a comfortable, if not a happy, life. When newspapers present ministers as modern versions of Kubla Khan, secretaries and others must be the happiest men alive. For they have the Good Life in a far greater measure, being accountable neither to Parliament nor to the public; with all their deadly devotion to files and their casual or habitual indulgence in drink, they run the affairs of state lugubriously. They need not resign; they get pensions; and they lose no time in joining firms on fat salaries as soon as they retire. Private secretaries and personal assistants, too, appointed on provincial or caste basis, according to the Delhi Telephone Directory, are safe. It is the show men that have been stripped; they are now like Madame Tussaud's wax figures without the wax.

The Good Life is a part of the social revolution, the emergence of the new and newer rich, led by business men, contact men and call girls. Public accountability does not extend to the private sector, though there is an occasional sensation like the Vivian Bose Report on some firms. These reports are only the garbage of the revolution. For a parallel, we have to recall the social change which accompanied the Industrial Revolution in Britain, when English and Scottish nobles came back with their loot from the Indies and revolutionized dinner habits, with rich spice-laden repasts and with liquor from France. In this process those who are accustomed to coffee and tea take to beer ; beer is replaced by wine or whisky. New Babylon's restaurants are increasing and almost every restaurant is increasingly full. Even communists do not want to be alienated from the Good Life ; they are to be found in the same places as the *bourgeoisie*, big and small, into which all small capitalists are being absorbed. Yet, the luxury of the period is more prodigal than refined. Among ministers at least, there is little refinement ; few of them entertain ; most of them are entertained ; few of them can talk on anything except their portfolios or interests. They are less Babylonian than denizens of the Diplomatic Enclave, but they are among the governing families which every ruling party breeds and they are on view more than diplomats.

Indian ministers have few perquisites, barring free accommodation, free electricity, free water and adequate allowance for tireless travelling. In the old days in Britain, each secretary of state received, on his appointment, a silver inkstand which he could hand down as a keepsake to his children ; this little perquisite was abolished ; and probably the only token of office which an outgoing minister can now take with him is his dispatch box, as in Test matches both winning and losing teams snatch at the stumps for souvenirs. Indian ministers have no dispatch boxes to take with them. The more adventurous of them write all their letters on official paper ; on whatever paper they are written, they go free if posted from the office. There is, however, the good side. Ministers' children must go to public schools ; personal cleanliness has become fashionable ; bedrooms are enlarged ; heaters are multiplied.

The causes of national intemperance at one stage in Britain were said to be the adulteration of liquor, the love of drink and the desire for more. In India the Good Life seems to have become similarly adulterated ; and there is a desire all round for more of it. There are no great political houses like Holland House and no great political hosts, but merchant princes play host to ministers and maintain luxurious guest houses. Most hospitality is generally at a lower level and on a wider scale, with the help of expense accounts, and this is some check on rigid class formation. Pitt destroyed the feudal character of the English peerage by declaring that every man who had an estate of ten thousand a year had a right to be a peer. He was supposed to have created a plebian aristocracy and blended it with the patrician oligarchy ; Indian princes are no longer patrician ; they are bankers, businessmen and politicians. Everything is business now, even the Good Life, and as business houses crash in a din of scandal, they may bring down any regime which they support. The Good Life may not be so good.

30. Goddess of Zinzka

DEVBA, the eighteen-year-old girl of Zinzka in the Saurashtra part of Gujarat who became the local goddess for a time, caused so much trouble for days that she was taken into police custody along with her accomplices, and for some time her divinity was *sub judice.* She was supposed to be a reincarnation of the goddess known as Bhavani and not a goddess in her own right. There was a made stampede to see her and over fifty persons at least were crushed to death. The people of Saurashtra are known for their religious-mindedness ; and the people of Zinzka in their numbness did not know whether what they were witnessing was an incarnation or impersonation. Devba was turning everything into saffron powder and there were rumours of miracles ; the people, too ready to believe, were stricken with faith, and faith is a commodity which can be traded. The authorities, caught unawares, thought there was a conspiracy, and Devba had to prove herself.

This was not for the first time that man's reason had been overpowered by the need for miracles. As long as the blind want to see, the deaf want to hear, the lame want to walk, the sick want to be whole, the lepers want to be clean, there will be search for the cure which the miracles of science cannot yet ensure. In 1950 Nepala of Rantalai, a boy tending cattle in a little-known village of Orissa, was built up into a miracle boy, and in the days-long stampede which followed, over five hundred people died of cholera. In 1954 hundreds died in a scramble at Allahabad in a mass religious gathering on the banks of the Ganga, aided by special means of locomotion and by paralysed police.

The primitiveness of creation still clings in many parts of the world and in many matters the people are still as virginal as the

Vestal Virgins. The soil in which many people try to think and act is superstition and it is difficult to define it; briefly, it is magic and religion, fertility rites and other ritual, a sum total of survival and accretion. In lands like Northern Rhodesia, where Alice Lenshina, posing to be a prophetess, created serious tribal unrest and trouble for the Government with fainting fits, there are even now totems growing into gods and goddesses. In India local popes dealing in sacred water, pavement palmists, cabalists, talisman-sellers, snake-worshippers, stone-worshippers and Satan worshippers, ministers tattooed with caste-marks, the wealthy who worship the goddess of wealth and the poor who worship the wealthy, gods in the crudest possible shape, their devotees with their obesity, gods who require ghee and camphor, are but a few of the forms of superstition. The high mountains are purgatories, and the Ganga and the Yamuna are waters of purification. To the drugged mind, or the empty mind, God appears in any form. The personalized god has been succeeded by the ungainly gods who can be seen at the cost of a ticket in any carnival. Fortunately for India, no priest or prophetess has created serious trouble like Alice Lenshina.

Industrialization is expected to destroy superstition and melt old gods into new metal. Four steel plants, huge fertilizer factories, aluminium factories, railway workshops, the Bhakra and other dams, and atomic reactors are not enough industrialization, but it may be the beginning of a new temper. Industrialization does not necessarily destroy gods. On the sixtieth storey of skyscrapers are centres of worship and mystic rites in America, where Mormons and Billy Graham are found necessary and where many people vote according to their religion and cannot forget their Irish descent or Scottish descent. The European mind, secular to a great degree, is now reconsidering the Lutheran doctrine about confession and communion, and the Song of Bernadette is still sung. In the Soviet Union, sputniks are semi-divine and missiles make a new totemism. The west cannot jeer at the Indian people's struggle to emerge from superstition to science. There is much that the people have to endure before they cease dying because of disease bred by pilgrim centres. In the transition period, there will be much mumbo-jumbo. Industrialization will make pilgrim centres more pestilential because railways and other modern means of communication will help pilgrims and their guides to congregate more speedily and irrationally to achieve quicker death. When the Indian people attain at least three-fourths rationality, even if they must cling one-fourth to superstition, they may get away from the grip of gods, old and new, and it is good that some gods or goddess are occasionally taken into custody by the ungodly but useful police.

31. *Sadhu Samaj of Chanakyapuri*

THE location of the Bharat Sadhu Samaj (the Indian Association of Holy Men) in Chanakyapuri, the city of Chanakya, which is the name for the Diplomatic Enclave in New Delhi, recalls the paradoxes that bedevil a country which is struggling to emerge from the medieval to the modern. People are asked to look forward and work for the future; many of them prefer to look backward and live in the past. Secularism and religious bigotry go together. The Taj is repaired, slums remain. Under non-co-operation, young men from Oxford and Cambridge gave up western dress and put on hand-spun, hand-woven cloth, which was called the livery of freedom; after freedom, old men in hand-spun, hand-woven cloth like to lounge in coffee houses painted like Paris cafés. After making laws in legislatures, legislators perform purificatory ceremonies. The state is laying emphasis on scientific progress, but astrology is being added to the sciences. Orthodoxy, caste-marks and vegetarianism mix easily with whisky and carnalism. Communists claim the right to coexistence, while sadhus, displaying a variegated hirsute culture, overrun the land.

There must have been sadhus throughout the ages and among them may have been a Francis of Assisi or a Bernard of Clairvaux. They could be embodiments not only of sweetness and light but of the spirit of sacrifice. It would be wrong to imagine them to be hairy creatures with beads round their necks and with a third eye hidden in their heads working for their salvation. There are other sets of people who probably deserve ridicule more than sadhus. Many of them at least perform miracles of abstinence or can be at least dull examples of plain living and high thinking with occasional parades at religious festivals. It is because they have broken their own code of obscurity, meditation and silent work and have come into the limelight that they do not appear to be the sadhus who were respected and ignored or were occasionally, if absent-mindedly, canonized by public opinion. They have organized themselves like a trade union and want to be licensed like homoeopaths; they hold conferences, pass resolutions and claim to be an economic force ready not only to spin but to toil. Encouraged to believe they are also a social order, they want to play a part in the progress of the country. They have proved themselves to be responsive and are prepared to render unto Caesar not only the things that are Caesar's but the things that are God's. This might not be a too distorted picture of the dialectical spiritualism which has been at work among them and which some might welcome as one way of saving the country from communism.

Sadhus are now organized as much as the Rotarians, that brotherhood of mutual reverence and professional multilateralism, the Freemasons who put on chains and meet in imposing structures of brick and mortar, or the Lions and other coteries of foreign inspiration. This may not be a new ritual of renunciation but rather the beginnings of a new snobbery. Sadhus, however, should not be confused with saints; they dwell on the lower summits of the spirit, not far from the base camp. They needed more than the modest 5-lakh-rupee structure amidst the embassy buildings which have been rising in the Diplomatic Enclave; they are free to have more mansions for the spirit, though they do not pretend to be monastic. At least they should not be allowed to invade homes except in the modest way in which astrologers invade homes to predict the unpredictable and comfort the afflicted. The Government, who have done much for ancient monuments, cannot treat associations of sadhus like scientific laboratories. The Panchen Lama, who made the insinuation that he had found the Stupa at Sarnath in a poor state, was less than just, unless he was as imaginative as the Indian visitor who, on seeing the Pyramids, expressed the regret that the Egyptian Government had not rebuilt them. The virtues of silence are celebrated at inordinate length in speech and song and the spirit might require to be housed in temples worthy of a Solomon. Dr. Radhakrishnan has said that a sadhu is one who is at peace with himself and spreads love. If something more than moral rearmament is expected of them, their association would consist of sadhus who are not at peace with themselves but will throw themselves into the social and economic struggle, without breaking their tradition of self-denial. In that evolution towards proletarianization, they might, while protesting against being called medievalists or revisionists, cease to be sadhus. It will be a gain for progress.

32. The Cold War

THE cold war crept into India, when it seemed Indians were achieving invulnerability of temper. It had begun when the war against fascism ended, and it is difficult to say whether international communism or international capitalism began it. Its ravages, more psychological than physical, are widespread, though the boundaries of countries have not changed because of it. There are, however, other changes; and one of them is aggression against men's minds abolishing all boundaries. It is a new process of human automation, in which intellectual integrity is difficult, and anything that remotely resembles intellectual activity is unwelcome because ideas, massed into a fervour of ideology, would not admit doubt or disbelief. There is no place for sceptics; everything is black or white.

The cold war is not without antecedents, but never was the intellect so passionately denied. It is done sometimes in the name of liberty and sometimes in the name of peace, but the result is shrinking of the human spirit. Every war has its apologists and historians and the rights and wrongs of the cold war are a difficult matter. There is hardly a parallel to this psychological, apart from military, division of the world. It has had some basis in rival systems of economic doctrine, but the cold war has developed some of life's new cruelties like character assassination, travesties of the truth, corruption of the mind and perversion of the heroic and martyr qualities of man.

McCarthyism was a manifestation as terrifying as witch-hunting. McCarthy and his friends were swearing bell, book and candle not from courage but from fear. Fear leads men into many false positions and McCarthy was in the ascendant in a nation's moment of fear. The fear was that the nation's security was threatened by

Soviet spies and their agents and there had been spy cases which laid the foundation for the fear. This led to persecution of a kind unprecedented since the conflict between Protestantism and Catholicism when people burnt each other in disputations over obscure passages in the Bible. Anyone who had touched anything communist or near-communist had to be unmasked and hunted. The past became a bogey and its unsuspecting victims were many. McCarthy created a hysteria which affected American policies, haunted by fear of the past and fear of the future. In the national self-distrust, nobody could claim to be a patriot unless he could prove it and many Americans became a prey to suspicion not only of the world but of themselves.

There were repercussions. If someone could be a communist in any sense, someone else could be an American stooge or agent. If the Soviet Union had planted spies in American atom stations, the State Department was sending spies in the guise of anthropologists and psychologists to all the dubious borders of the world. The agents of the Soviet view of life or of the American view of life may have had little to do with communism or monopoly capitalism, but they planted the seed of suspicion wherever they went. Peace became anathema because it was supposed to be communist and freedom because it was supposed to be American. It was when increasing numbers of Americans, including senators, could go about snooping in Moscow or increasing numbers of Soviet citizens, including Khrushchev and Mikoyan, could go up and down Manhattan that McCarthyism began to lose its appeal.

The state of fright which was becoming outmoded elsewhere has developed among Indians. It is difficult to say who started it. Character assassination has been in vogue for some years as a means of promoting the interests of some country or ideology, and foreign embassies have taken part in the business. In such a mass neurosis it is difficult to build individual or national character. There have been subterfuges, holiday jaunts, rest cures and other attractions; there can be the more attractive aid programmes to influence national policies. Such corruption wholly corrupts small nations, but in a big nation, it can weaken the people's strength, and divide them. India's policy of non-alignment did not mean a ban on ideological differences or on advocacy of alignment. If non-alignment conferred freedom on the people, it did not mean a licence for witch-hunting. Revolutions, if they are wanted, cannot be brought about by intrigues, and intriguing is not ideology. India cannot become one of the lesser countries of South-east Asia nor New Delhi, however infested and open a city, a Kalimpong. But the Indian mind is besieged, and to remain Indian without ceasing to be pro-American or pro-Soviet demands intellectual courage and integrity.

33. Foreign Policy

FOREIGN policy tradition is yet in the making in India. When Gandhi said that he wanted India to keep her windows open to the winds of the world, he may not have thought of the winds which had been blowing in for centuries in the physical and the historical sense. In the old days, Indian rulers had to fight invaders from the north-west, whenever they were not busy fighting among themselves. The Moguls could not forget their Central Asian origins. British India had relations only with the Near East and the Middle East, though in the Boxer Rebellion, Indian troops were transported as far as China. The Indians throughout could be said to be peace-loving, like peoples everywhere else probably, but they were less troubled about what foreign policy was. Free India's foreign policy grew from subject India's foreign policy; it was an amplification of old Congress resolutions, which demanded freedom for subject peoples and peace among nations. There was vision, and with clarity of vision, there might be aberrations but there could be no longer adventurism.

India's foreign policy has had to be contained. She is big; her population is numerous; her economy is underdeveloped; even after Partition, she is one of the biggest Muslim countries in the world. She seemed to enjoy the protection of the Himalayas but only till 1962. There could be no doubt about her interests, but interests alone do not make policy. The meagre contribution which the several parties in Parliament make, in debate after debate on foreign policy, shows that there are no differences on interests too and that, without a long tradition, the tradition-makers have an advantage, while the dissenters or the trouble-makers, as Mr. A. J. P. Taylor would call them, are found foundering. The dissenters of today become the traditionalists of tomorrow and responsibility in office overrides the opposition tendency to oppose. That was how Gladstone got entangled in Egypt, how latter-day Little-England Liberals could not avoid supporting the Boer War, and how peace-loving chancellors like Lloyd George became great war-time prime ministers. There has been a consistency of outlook in Indian policy, and whatever its failures, there is yet no alternative policy except the half-hearted alternative of alignment. The present period may rank with that of Jefferson and Monroe in the United States and that of Chatham in Britain for its uncharted courses.

Non-alignment, of which India is the author and main exponent, does not mean what many want it to mean. It is only one aspect of policy, not the whole of policy. It means that India does not want to be aligned to either of the two big military blocs, as long as they exist and divide the world. It does not mean that India is not committed to any cause. African freedom had no more committed champion than India and the 1956 attack on Egypt was nowhere else abhorred so much, even officially, as in India. A country like India cannot afford to be unsteady and can have no eternal friends or eternal enemies, but it need not act from fear or irresponsibility, like smaller countries; it has a heavy load of national tradition to carry. Now, when non-alignment has preserved an era of peace and is respected, the aligned nations themselves are not as aligned as they were and the meaning of non-alignment is changing. Geography affects policies powerfully, as it does in the case of the smaller communist countries of Europe. Thailand, for instance, has derived much from India and China, through centuries, and many things Thai are either Indian or Chinese, but the political-minded Thai for that very reason must dislike India and China as big neighbours, not merely because of their policies. There is little reason why Iran and Afghanistan should differ strongly except that Iran has a long coast and Afghanistan is land-locked and must look up to the tableland in the north and the historical connection with Samarkand and Bokhara. Any country, not threatened by aggression or subversion, can find it to be of advantage to be non-aligned, though only a big country like India could have given significance to non-alignment.

India became free when true nationalism could mean true internationalism, and for years, Indians had imbibed the international outlook at Jawaharlal Nehru's insistence. Even without direct relations with other countries, they admired the League of Nations and deplored its decay, watched with anxiety the Italian invasion of Abyssinia, the civil war in Spain, and the Japanese attack on Manchuria. There were no more ardent anti-fascists. After the war, among their first preferences was the United Nations. There is more allegiance to the idea of international law and morality in India, where the ancients prayed for peace for the whole world, than in any other country. For a people who have no memories of hatred and have forgotten even the bitterness of British rule, it is not difficult to mix with all the odd assortment of people who come uninvited or invited. Only in one way are the people aligned, whatever governments and political parties may do; they are aligned to socialist reconstruction because that seems to be the way for prosperity and for peace.

Indian critics of their country's foreign policy have thought that there has been too great a meddlesome interest in international affairs. This was largely a realistic interest in freedom and peace, and now when almost the whole world is free, the interest in peace remains. With the United States and the Soviet Union closer to India than before, alignment has fewer critics now. The criticism now is that India has not cultivated Asian and African countries successfully; this is to forget that each country has its own interests to serve and it could afford to be neutral in the cause of other countries. With sovereign equality, Nepal is the equal of India and sovereign; so is Ceylon, or Dahomey, or the Upper Volta. They are not unfriendly, but if the critics want them to choose between India and Pakistan or between India and China, when the choice is not so awful and no such choice need be made, they are suggesting impossible tests. There are noisy differences within NATO and within the Soviet bloc and Britain cannot find allies who will always vote with her.

India has probably no diplomatic finesse or cunning, but every

Indian diplomat cannot be expected to be a Talleyrand or a Metternich, when diplomacy is decided far behind the conference table and has to be backed by economic or military strength. The Chinese attack is making India a power among powers, but she does not want to go through the costly and exhausting process of militarization. Some strength is necessary when a big country has to assume big responsibilities, or even defend itself. Most Indians are more international-minded than ever, for it seems peace abroad and peace at home are necessary for progress and the impact of international developments on internal affairs is made clear impressively even to isolationists. It is no use asking Indian newspapers in even the smaller towns to give increasingly more local news, for newspaper readers are insatiably interested in what happens all over the world, even in remote places in the Congo.

34. Multi-racial Commonwealth

IT WAS said that it was India that made the British Empire imperial; for some years, it seemed, it was India that made the Commonwealth what it was. The Dominions had been constitutionally described as crowned republics; with India, a republic without royalty was added. The Commonwealth represents nearly a quarter of the population of the world and India contributes most of it. But the Commonwealth is no longer British or Indian or Asian in influence or authority; it is also African and Caribbean, and it has been found useful to look at world problems not only from London, New Delhi, or Kuala Lumpur, but from Mombasa or Kingston. In a multi-racial association, member countries now discuss racial questions and assert racial equality. This is possible because they are members of the United Nations, enjoy sovereign equality, each free to follow its interests and to differ from the rest on any problem. The British sovereign is the head but the link is symbolic. The common bond is that all the new members were till recent years British colonies, and when more colonies, including Pitcairn in the Pacific with its ninety inhabitants, will be free, the Commonwealth will contain more members than Marlborough House can accommodate.

The search for commonness in the Commonwealth was becoming desperate. Some things had been common; the English language, which is the first language in all countries and will hereafter at least be the second in some, Shakespeare, whose quater-centenary has strengthened memories of his supreme genius, and parliamentary institutions. The English language has not always been a uniting force, for it has not prevented the separation of the United States, and Eire, from Britain, and parliamentary democracy has been discarded in some countries, which prefer presidents in plebiscitary conditions. The British, forced to prefer the Commonwealth to the Common Market, have devised new commonness, besides aid and trade and the Commonwealth Parliamentary Association, new development projects, co-operation in education and satellite communication, and a Commonwealth foundation. A Commonwealth secretariat, which looked remote, is now much wanted, and London is no longer considered a too dominating position for it. The Commonwealth is still an awkward camel, but it seems to work.

India's membership of the Commonwealth has to be defended sometimes, but it is recognized as not inconsistent with India's freedom. The Commonwealth, which is becoming an association of peoples as much as of governments, has been a force for peace and will never be a military bloc. Queen Elizabeth's visit to India in 1961 recalled the long and chequered history of Indo-British relations, and what could sum up these relations better than that the Queen witnessed the Republic Day parade and pageant? The first and last time a reigning British sovereign had visited India was when George V was crowned in Delhi in 1912 amidst tumultuous splendour; after the First World War, the Duke of Connaught inaugurated the Montagu–Chelmsford Constitution, and the Duke of Windsor also made his troubled tour as the Prince of Wales. In 1959 Prince Philip moved about modestly in a short scouting expedition. There will be no more of the Delhi Durbars where magnificently bejewelled princes and native knights of chivalry walked with their backs to the audience in ridiculous obeisance. Queen Elizabeth's predecessors ruled and reigned over India; she is somewhat remote as the symbolic head of the Commonwealth.

British sovereigns were little more than long-haired miniatures in the crowded portrait gallery of history books. Almost every Indian schoolboy knew Alfred, though not why he was called "the Great", William the Conqueror, Henry V, haloed by Shakespeare, the terrible Tudor who married many women and somewhat resembled Charles Laughton, and the first Elizabeth. The story of the Stuarts repels, unrelieved by the gloomy gusto of Cromwell and the Puritans, but now almost every book on the Restoration is seeking to rehabilitate Charles II. As historians repeat themselves more than history repeats itself, George III was a madman, George IV a rake and William IV a fool. At any rate India had little to do with them, or even with the early Victoria. It was in her later years that she became the symbol of an imperial benevolence which was brought out in its widowed dignity in marble and enthroned in parks and buildings. Victoria the Good took some interfering interest in India as in foreign, affairs, but except for 1857–8, the days passed as peacefully in India as in Britain. Edward VII and George V had no sympathy for Indian nationalism and did not care to conceal their views; they were ignorant and courageous enough, but they could not but mumble agreement in the end to the stately progress of reforms. George VI's attitudes were not known at least to Indians, and as for the combined house of Windsor-Mountbatten, Indians have had no historical or personal grudges.

Queen Elizabeth was in India when royalty in Britain had been modernized. It had, of course, not been deglamorized as in Sweden, Norway or Greece, but the irreverence of men like Altrincham and Muggeridge had left royalty unscathed. Whatever the lingering ceremonial, royalty had lost a large part of its old Ruritanian flavour. George V was probably the first modern, more of a man and less of a king, who not only indulged in plebian gestures like his father, but moved among the people like a genial squire. Queen Elizabeth had been brought up under an exact routine and the privilege of being sovereign was subject to the performance of duties prescribed by the people. The task of receiving her was not exacting for a people capable of disorderly enthusiasm. There was constitutional significance about the visit of the head of the Commonwealth, but Queen Elizabeth was also the sovereign of the British people, representing their history, their culture, their strength, their orderliness and their sense of discipline. To the British people, it was a Commonwealth occasion, though interest in India is usually confined to Caxton Hall and to old civil servants ruminating over lost empires. The Indian people, too, woke up to the wholesomeness of the Commonwealth concept, and to the importance of India. Queen Elizabeth renewed a heritage, something more than the trade figures which British Chancellors recite on Indo-British occasions.

35. War on the Border

INDIANS have reason to regret their peaceableness. They thought they had escaped two world wars and had won freedom without violence. Peace was their shelter. It was not so much peace in the world as a kind of peace of mind, a smoky smugness of spirit. War may have made them whole if it had come to them before they were free ; it would have shattered lethargy and the social system, and made them scarred and tough. Too much spirituality, real or false, in a world still raw with violence was not good. The First World War was remote ; even Mesopotamia with its battlefields was a blessed word and nothing more ; Indian soldiers were withdrawn from Flanders' fields before they could win more Victoria Crosses. The Second World War came near to them but receded. But India had all the evil effects of war with none of its heroism, nothing remotely suggesting the British spirit after Dunkirk, the Soviet mood after Stalingrad, or the French resurgence after capitulation. In the freedom movement, spirits were uplifted spirits, but it often meant a hide-and-seek with the non-violent nature of British colonialism. When freedom came, it was unsullied by the impurities which make its ends sullied. There was no need to follow the haphazard opportunism of peoples moulded by wrong means. All these years, it seemed means and ends were the same, but now national security demands that people become stern, purposeful, nationalistic.

The conflict which China forced on the Indian people has abridged the nation-building process. If a nation was the unity of the people, the Indian people were one, and as a nation lives and acts like a man, they are likely to be very human in their reactions. They are not a nation in arms, nor a nation with a bloodshot vision. The history of the nationalist struggle and the self-possession which it bred saved them from narrow-mindedness, and Indian leadership showed self-confidence and clarity of vision. The emergency imposed on all the conditions of war-time restraint, but discipline was the basis of defence, and it would be proof of the reality of democratic faith, if India developed discipline from liberty. The release of reservoirs of emotion and of loyalty for which the nation stood gladdened the Indian people and their friends. It was a young nation which had risen in self-defence, though Indian civilization is old, and there is a chance of it making fewer mistakes than other nations. Whatever the excesses in some places, there was rejoicing in this moment of self-realization. It was a more complete lyric of a nation's self-expression than even the lyricism of the non-co-operation movement.

The Indian people tried their best to avoid war in the belief that peace at home and abroad was desperately necessary and that there were moral equivalents to war. They lost territory in the process; in the end their very security was threatened. War is failure of human wisdom and not inevitable. But there are worse things than war—sloth, fear, smugness, pacifism, dishonour, surrender. China forced a people who had been appalled by Munich to realize that acquiescence under insult is not the way to escape war. So, though some people may think that war is not good because it spoils conversation and others may think it good because it puts a nation in uniform, it could not be avoided, and it may not be a short war. It is not merely an army that has to be kept ready but a nation, and no nation can afford to make the same mistake twice. It is not enough to depend on what has been called the notable ferocity of non-combatants. Almost everybody realizes the need for guiding the energies of the people, saved from the dissipations of peace time. The confrontation on the border may not lead to war or peace; it may lead to the strain of neutralized feeling. The Chinese are accustomed to think in terms of centuries and Indians, too, can come to terms with time.

36. Revolutions in Conflict

INDIA and China are in contact with each other not only along the two-thousand-mile Himalayan border but throughout South-east Asia. The invisible border is also important, for it has been the meeting place of two civilizations for centuries and now of two revolutions, representing two chosen ways of life. In Chinese conditions, communism was destined to succeed. The Soviet Union with its military might was in the background, the long-drawn-out civil war left the people without a strong national government, the Kuomintang regime was rotting with corruption, and the Japanese in their retreat left arms for the communists to gather. Mao Tse-tung, breaking the orthodox doctrines of Marxism-Leninism, organized the revolutionary possibilities of the peasants in degrading feudal conditions, and had been running a government for ten years in Yenan. There was no defence of any kind against communism. Confucianism and Buddhism, with their emphasis on ethics, had impressed on the people a secular outlook which made them accept any political doctrine which promised a strong government. The human material was malleable and could be moulded by a political party with a ready-made and wholesale philosophy. When Emperor Shih Huang Ti, two centuries before Christ, unified the country and imposed one script and one language, whatever may be the dialects, he made it possible two thousand years later for communism to operate successfully in such a vast country. Nowhere is the temperature high any time in the year. India, with a stubborn social structure in which religion is interwoven, with a broad basis of unified and orderly government for nearly a hundred years, and with a climate, in which even Lenin would have wilted into a local revolutionary, is different. The

Indian people are not clay for political potters; even if class ever re-emerges from caste, they may remain somewhat individualistic.

Chinese civilization, like Indian civilization, is ancient, massive, and continuous, and it is difficult to say which is older. The Chinese have older records, while the proof of Indian antiquity lies in Mohenjo-doro. Among Chinese philosophers, Confucius, with his emphasis on an ideal society, has had a permanent influence. Buddhism was taken to China through Sinkiang along the caravan routes probably in the early years of the Christian era and its influence lasted for nearly a thousand years. Buddhist scholars from China and India exchanged visits. Buddhist books in Pali were translated into Chinese. Buddhist temples and statues were built in several places and even rulers and noblemen became converts. Early in the twelfth century, Confucianism reasserted itself and Buddhism lost its influence. The common sense of Confucius had a greater appeal than the metaphysics of the Buddha to the materialistic, pragmatic Chinese mind. Without amounting to a religion, Confucianism prescribed a way of life in this world, discarding other-worldliness. After a challenge from Western civilization in the nineteenth century, the Confucian way became an easy passport to the communist way of life. Like India, China seemed unchanging, with no change in the modes of production, but without the measured liberalism of British rule, China was riper for violent revolution.

The first mood of China under communist rule was inevitably warlike, with the Kuomintang threatening invasion from Formosa and with constant danger of subversion. But soon the Chinese Revolution put on the smile of a Cheshire cat behind the benevolent looks of the fatherhood of Mao Tse-tung, not only China's leader but China's poet, philosopher and military genius. It seemed the Chinese leaders had preserved the humanism and moralism of Confucian tradition. There was indoctrination everywhere but the doctrine was good, like loyalty to country and care of public property. The people were to be persuaded, not coerced, and there were furious campaigns of conversion from corruption of every kind. The past was not to be repudiated wholly. Tang horses were repaired, Ming pottery was popularized, Peking opera was used to present the revolutionary significance of old legends. The bells were ringing in temples. Behind the drab uniformity of grey, in which ministers and clerks were clothed to proclaim social equality, every gesture spoke of centuries-long civilization. Landlords were deprived of excess land but not liquidated physically. Even by 1952, there were few co-operative farms. The Chinese Revolution, it seemed, had learnt from the mistakes of the Russian Revolution. A superior civilization was showing what it could make of Marxism–Leninism by adding the Thought of Mao.

The faith of the Chinese in the superiority of their race has been transmitted under Chinese communism, and it is seen in the attitude to other countries, including communist countries. After the first phase of recuperation, collectivization proceeded at a furious pace, and co-operative farms soon led not only to big leaps but to communes. There are various estimates of the triumphs and failures, but the tight regimentation of 650 million people, in which the women do a good share of the work, is a new type of totalitarianism. The schism in international communism is not a matter of doctrine but of clash of national interests, and what the rest of the world, including communist countries, is afraid of is the survival value of 650 million regimented people in a nuclear war.

The relations between India and China, which began with the introduction of Buddhism in China, about A.D. 67, were remote till the disappearance of Tibet as a buffer state brought China to the Indian border. Chinese aims are known to be ideological and not merely military. If the Chinese had not invaded India, co-existence would have seemed possible, and for several years Chinese leaders wanted India and other non-communist Asian countries to go their own way, if only they did not play the part of agents of the United States. In South-east Asia, millions of Chinese live amidst the populations claiming to be citizens of China and are a perpetual source of subversion. India had colonies once in South-east Asia and traces of Indian civilization are still strong in Thailand, Cambodia and Java. Thailand illustrates a dual cultural allegiance. The *Ramayana* is the Old Testament and Buddhism is the New Testament of the Thais and Thai life has been deeply influenced by the Chinese. Yet the Thais have reason to dislike the Chinese because they have gone communist and the Indians because they are not members of SEATO. India's sponsorship of China, for realistic and not ideological considerations, did much to confuse this part of the world more than others, and small countries, which do not trust big countries, are not prepared to choose between China and India. Chinese strength and its assertion are feared, while the Indian way of life and Indian diplomacy appear soft and idealistic. Whether there is to be competition or co-existence between the influence that India or China can wield, it is not a rivalry merely between Indian and Chinese interests. India represents certain values and a democratic way of life, in spite of revolutionary urges, and China represents a communism which is at war even with the rest of international communism. It is a conflict between two revolutions.